# SELL MORE
### *and*
# SLEEP AT NIGHT

"The insights earned and learned in these pages
will help transform any sales culture and increase
the productivity of any sales organization."

"A refreshing, practical approach to
increasing sales in any industry."

"Fact-based strategic and tactical action steps that will leave
you wondering why this has never been written before."

# SELL MORE
## *and*
# SLEEP AT NIGHT

### Developing Relationships
### with Emotional Intelligence
### to Increase Sales

## John Richard Pierce Jr.

Foreword from Emotional Intelligence expert and best-selling author
### Frances Johnston, PhD

**To**

Meghan, John, and Thomas, who inspire and fill
your mom and me with pride every day

Shawn

Mom and Dad, for being awesome parents

Fran, the reason this book was written

*JRP*

# Contents

## Part 3: The Sales Process

## Part 4: The Diversified Sourcing Strategy

## Part 5: Meeting with Your Client or Prospect

## Part 6: Evaluating Why Sales Are Not Increasing

## Part 7: Closing Thoughts

## Part 8: Bonus Coverage

# Foreword

## from emotional intelligence expert and best-selling author Frances Johnston, PhD

Every day we are invited to enter into relationships where we exchange money for services or things. We decide to trust someone or a product. We calculate whether the thing we are being sold will meet our needs or help us in some way. This book is about what happens in that experience. Reading this book will enable you to successfully establish the kind of professional practice you want: a successful one where you can bring genuine value to other people with integrity and heart.

Think to the last time you were sold something important. I am not talking about buying—I am talking about being sold on a product by a person. Buying and being sold on a product are two very different things. Buying doesn't necessarily have anything to do with anyone other than you and the product. You can buy a billion things on the Internet, for instance. But being sold involves communication, a relationship (however brief), and an act of interpersonal influence. You may have had real reservations about the product—too expensive, don't need it, etc.—but somehow you end up buying it. Chances are you were sold on the person before you were sold on the product, and that's why relationships matter in sales.

The first part of the title is "Sell More." Relationships help you sell more, and self-aware people with the emotional intelligence to manage themselves and understand the motives, needs, and feelings of others can create deeper, stickier relationships. The second part of the title, "and Sleep at Night," has two meanings, at least for me. The first, sales-related one implies that when you are more successful, you will worry less and be able to sleep soundly because you are achieving your goals, closing deals, and feeling successful. The second meaning, though, is that you are sleeping more soundly because you are selling with integrity. You are influencing people, they are trusting you, and you are providing them with a service or product that helps *them* achieve *their* goals, not simply helping *you* achieve *your* goals.

For the last twenty years, I have had the privilege of working with organizations and leaders, helping to increase their self-awareness, influence, and productivity by creating strong relationships and positive work environments. It is how I came into a relationship with the author of this book, John Pierce. I met John when he was a leader in a major financial services organization, and he was tasked with helping other people achieve the success he had when he sold products and services. He was very successful, very driven, and not that into slowing down to reflect on his purpose and values. He knew his targets, he was relentless himself, and was a product of a very successful sales organization that had campaigns, trips, and incentives worked out to the penny. He was also searching for something deeper.

The financial industry was a different place twenty years ago than it is now. John has had to adapt and change as an industry founded on relationship selling shifted to selling products—a stock, a bond, a fund—based on the firm's intelligence via those relationships, and now to a time when individuals can go onto the Internet and buy it themselves. And now more recently, the public is not only independent ("I can do it myself") but suspicious of the industry after the financial crisis of 2008 ("So tell me again, why do I need a broker?"). You need a good financial services professional because you need experienced, reasoned advice! And we only take advice from people we trust.

John and his colleagues in the industry always knew that relationships matter. Sure, some may have lost their way, but the best never did because they cared about their clients. They used their empathy and great social skills to help their clients weather the crisis. John has worked to refine his insights about the importance of leadership and relationships into tried and tested processes and practices. That is what you will find in this book.

John and I have had many wonderful conversations about our work and approaches. We have discussed the importance of emotional intelligence in all leadership roles and how it is particularly essential in sales. As this book, *Sell More and Sleep at Night*, will show you, John knows that the best salespeople are self-aware, relationship-oriented individuals who are deeply interested in their clients' successes. They start with the premise "I want you to be successful because I know you. I can see how I have something that will help you, and therefore I feel compelled to lead you in an authentic, resonant way toward a new future."

Relationship selling goes beyond emotional intelligence to a disposition of being other-focused to such a degree that you are in tune with others' emotions, hopes, and desires—and with how you can meet those needs. There are more and more books about relationship selling. What this book offers is the insight that relationships begin with *you*. You can't change anyone but yourself, so working on yourself is the best place to begin your journey of relationship selling; whether you are new to it or an old hand, there is much to be learned because the focus is on you, and you are always growing and adapting. We learned this concept in the leadership field when, in the late 1990s, new scientific research began to emerge from neuroscience that placed leadership development squarely in the focus on self-awareness and emotional self-management. Leadership is a relational act, like selling, and so we need to deeply understand what we leaders are bringing to the leader-follower equation.

Emotional intelligence starts with self-awareness—the ability to recognize your own emotions, needs, and desires. With such a foundation, you can develop the ability to recognize the emotional reality of others and to react in a way that builds strong relationships and leads to successful, positive influence. In short, emotional intelligence is comprised of the following four elements: self-awareness, self-management, social awareness, and relationship management. All of these skills play crucial roles in the sales relationship.

The starting point is self-awareness. We have known that since the beginning of recorded history; it was the directive at the Temple of Apollo at Delphi. This book invites you into a practical, persistent journey of self-awareness. Self-awareness goes beyond simply recognizing your own emotions and physical sensations; it includes being in touch with your personal values, your motivations, and your unique and noble purpose in the world. Why do you sell? What are your motivations? Do you really want to help people? Are you honest enough to say no, if that is your answer? Emotional intelligence doesn't say you must be kind; it invites you to be honest and authentic. We trust your values will align if you take the time to analyze them. In my twenty years of helping leaders like John help themselves grow to the next level of their potential, I can honestly say that 99.9 percent of people are good people who want to help. And that includes you!

Emotional intelligence also involves being able to recognize and manage emotions in others, which largely stems from our ability to do so within ourselves. Not surprisingly, these skills can only be honed through experience—and through building and maintaining effective relationships with others. Over the years, my relationship with John has played an important role in helping him know what motivates him, what his dreams are, where he gets in his own way, and much more. He learned through talking things out with me and with his mentors, from taking risks, and, most importantly, from reflecting on what worked, what didn't work and how he felt. "Sleeping at night" comes from feeling okay with what you did during the day, and that requires authenticity and execution. You have to work the plan, and you have to be a good person while you do.

The relationship between self-awareness and relationships is cyclical. The stronger our relationships are, the more self-aware we become as we observe our effect on others and how it is reflected to us through their behavior. Self-awareness, then, enables us to have deeper, stronger, and more meaningful relationships. John's book demonstrates that all people and all relationships work this way, and it provides an invaluable resource for the serious sales professional. It offers guidance and practical methods to enhance self-awareness and build stronger relationships. This book shows that relationship selling *is* the most effective and satisfying approach to sales.

Whether it is in your own self-exploration or in building relationships with others, you can join John in exploring what it means to take a holistic view of life and to place dreams and a vision of your ideal future at the center of your personal and professional learning plan. It is really a virtuous cycle to realize that when you are working toward your dreams in a self-aware and relationship-oriented way, you will be a better leader and salesperson. There can be balance and partnership.

Throughout *Sell More and Sleep at Night*, John helps you to understand and manage the sales process by walking you through each step. Relationship selling is not a cookie-cutter approach—it means tailoring these practices to your own business and the needs of your customers. This is why it rests on the core idea of knowing yourself and deeply understanding your social world, from potential clients to current clients, to the competition, and to the industry as a whole.

In addition to his invaluable guidance on self-awareness and relationships, John uses his years of successful experience in sales to show that success is built on a foundation of emotional intelligence, and he provides practical advice on how to demonstrate it in the sales relationship. All the heart and empathy in the world won't help you unless you have a clear process with steps and actions. John gives you this and more. Ah, but you won't work that process unless you have the ability, like John, to persist and actually manage yourself into setting up the system and following through. John has spent twenty years developing, refining, adapting, and honing the process as he has taught and implemented it in sales organizations of thousands of people. I have learned this process from John, and it has helped me along with those other thousands of people. I know you will benefit too.

The clear steps and process John offers is the real meat of the book, but it doesn't work without that special sauce of self-awareness and relationships. I join John in wanting you to be successful, because I believe in the power of resonant sales relationships. I don't just want you to follow his incredibly helpful tips and process—I want you to be happy. John has delivered to you, and offers to you for a ridiculously low price, a career's worth of sales advice. He will create a relationship with you through this book. That is one of the things that will help you work the plan!

John is always learning from experience, and he has mastered the sales process over his career; he is a true sales leader. One last thing: John is super smart. You will see that in his persistent wish to help us all with our vocabulary. He is fun. This book is fun. You can learn a sales process by learning more about yourself—your values, your dreams, your strengths, and the things about yourself around which you need to organize. Your customers will be enriched by the new way you listen and relate to them. It doesn't take more time, it takes more awareness. Enjoy the journey.

*—Fran*

# Thank You

Thank you for purchasing this book. I truly appreciate your purchase. I genuinely want this book to help you in your current job. More importantly, I trust this book will help you to develop better relationships over time. Better relationships help in work and in everyday life.

# About This Book

This book came about after a sit-down with my coach, friend, and mentor, Fran. After working with each other for years, Fran said, "It's time for you to write a book." We were discussing what I wanted to do, and she said, "It's in your hands." I didn't wish I would write a book—I began a journey that led me to finishing this book. I had to implement many of the concepts about which I've written. The most time-consuming part of the writing process was forcing myself to take time to think about what would benefit you and what was really valuable to me (and thus, potentially, you). I thought about people who have taught me large and small lessons. I thought about successes and failures I have seen or experienced. From there I created a game plan to get this in your hands. The game plan I created to write this book is similar to the game plan I need you to write in order to help you develop stronger and more meaningful relationships. These relationships will help you achieve what you want over the next ten years of your life.

I have been blessed to work in the financial services industry for over twenty years, and I am still in this industry in various capacities. I started years ago with a phone and a directory of numbers, earned my way into senior leadership positions, and led sales teams for financial services, sourcing, and product sales. In each role I learned valuable lessons that helped me at work and in life. At each company I also made lifelong friends who have helped me in my yet uncompleted journey. What I have learned along the way is documented in these pages.

Look at this book as a *manifesto* or guide of topics to help you not only sell more but become a more complete leader. The book's intent is to provide the tools to supercharge your growth so that you don't have to spend the next few years figuring it out on your own.

The contents of this book are closely interrelated and connected to help you excel at whatever you do. Clearly some topics may be more helpful than others for your line of work, however please don't discount a subject until you have read the entire book and found the connection points.

The topics in this book are both strategic and tactical. As you read through the pages, you will be provided with some clear directions that have been proven to work over time. You will also read topics that relate to high-level strategy. The strategic topics will need more thought and contemplation because the implications will differ for each individual.

The contents of this book are based on having a positive outlook on various areas of your life. Optimism will never replace hard work, however it will help you through times of hard work without any apparent results. The people you read about in this book are optimists of the highest level because they have learned that pessimism has minimal value.

When you see things repeated in this book, it is on purpose. Things get repeated because people need to hear, read, or see something multiple times before it sticks.

No *hubris* is intended, so please pay attention to the key topics and make your investment in this book pay off.

## Vocabulary*

Manifesto: a written statement of the beliefs

Hubris: an extreme and unreasonable feeling of pride and confidence in yourself

---

* All definitions in this book are from the Cambridge Dictionaries Online (http://dictionary.cambridge.org).

# The Ask

As you read this book, I ask you to do a few things. I believe if you do these things, you can maximize the value of this work. I know that when I read a book, sometimes I try to plow through it, and I miss out on the value that could help me. I truly want you to realize the value of my twenty-plus years of experience.

## Reflect

Please spend time reflecting on each of these quick-paced chapters. You are so busy with your day-to-day life that it is difficult to reflect on transformational topics you may read, hear, or watch. We absorb something and move on. Please slow down; take your time as you read this book and truly reflect on the content. Reflect on what differs in your short-term and long-term approach to your job and life, compared to the best practices and ideas presented in this book. At the end of most sections, there is an activity to consider. Instead of charging to the next chapter, please consider working on each activity.

## Believe

Not many people really care about what you think. People care about what you believe. After each chapter, make a note to yourself. If you believe something has value, highlight the section, make a note of the page, and then revisit and reflect on the topic. Success depends on your belief in yourself and how you express that belief. You will see the word "genuine" throughout this book; it is a simple word to say but is complex in its depth. What you believe and how you come across to your clients and prospects will help determine whether you are awesome at developing relationships or are just average.

## Implement

Purchasing this book and getting all fired up is a waste of your intellectual capital and time. If you need to change some things in your life, now is the time to do it. Avoid the trap of the three-day seminar that gets you completely excited and feeling like you can become the best salesperson on the planet. You get home only to realize, once the euphoria wears off, that you wasted a lot of time and money and didn't change a darn thing. Select the topics that you will *implement* after you have spent time reflecting on each topic, and then decide how to execute based on strategic and tactical ideas in these pages.

## Consider Integrity

You need to be comfortable in your own skin. You also need to live your life in a way that enables you to sleep at night as you sell more stuff. We look in the mirror as we brush our teeth in the morning. We may end up selling a lot of stuff. If we don't do it the right way, we may have a nice short-term gain or a nice paycheck, but the negative ripple effects can be very damaging. This book provides the road map with some very prescriptive recommendations. You need to implement these recommendations with *integrity* for long-term success. That integrity also allows you to smile at the person in the mirror each morning.

I am not going to sell more stuff for you. If your intent is to read a book and then have something magically happen, you will be very disappointed. What is provided are fact-based learnings that have come at great pain, expense, and a lot of fun over the last twenty years.

The lessons can be applied to any industry or to any company because they are lessons with examples from real people.

As we start this journey together, let's have some fun. Spend time thinking, contemplating, and acting to change things. Along the way you will see the theme of doing things the right way. Doing things the right way is really important; there are plenty of business reasons as to why the right way makes sense for you as a salesperson of your company. Longer term, doing things the right way allows you to put your exhausted head down on your pillow at night, have a little smile, and sleep like a baby without a care in the world.

Here is one of the first big ideas in the book. I don't care what role you have; everyone is a salesperson. Even if you don't sell a specific widget, think about sales as influencing or driving change. Everything we do in life is sales. Do you want to sell more? If you answered yes, let's start!

## Vocabulary

Implement: to put a plan or system into operation

Integrity: the quality of being honest and having strong moral principles

# Selling Stuff

Think about a barbell.

The barbell has two separate ends. Think of each end as the two parts of this book. One part comprises the tactical action steps that you might consider; the other part, the more cerebral part, focuses on your strategic approach. Typically you develop your strategy and then implement via tactics. These concepts work together, and both have value.

When you read about tactics, you may believe I am being too prescriptive. Please take a leap of faith when you think I am being too detailed. I say this because I believe these tactics will help you. I have seen this approach help countless leaders who were really good but couldn't transform into really awesome.

The other end of the tactical barbell is the other end of the spectrum, the strategy. Changing a *strategic* vision will cause discomfort in a company but can lead to *transformational* change. Big ideas, high concepts, and bold visions are the substance of what makes our country amazing. Being able to clearly articulate the strategy behind a vision, concept, or big idea is where a lot of people get tripped up and fall short of acceptance.

The strategic parts of this book require you to use your brain. The strategic parts are not prescriptive; they require you to take a blank canvas and paint what is an ideal for you, your family, and your clients and prospects. You change things by providing the strongest foundation to stand your idea upon and then helping people to understand the idea and agree with you. That may not be selling a product, but it is selling an idea in which you believe. That makes you a salesperson.

## Vocabulary

Strategic: a long-range plan for achieving something or reaching a goal; the skill of making such plans

Transformation: a complete change in the appearance or character of something or someone

# Case Study: Mike—Life's Lessons

Let's revisit and *visualize* the barbell. As you contemplate your job and personal life, there are simple tactical lessons to learn and meaningful strategic lessons by which to live. Both are important. Both need to be paid attention to. In this section I will discuss some tactical suggestions and two meaningful strategic concepts.

Mike was my first boss in a leadership role on the East Coast, and he taught me a lot. Unfortunately, as a young person, I didn't appreciate all he tried to teach me. A lot of times I heard, but I didn't listen. As you grow and evolve, hopefully you will have great bosses who make a lasting impact on you. As someone makes an impact, attempt to listen to him or her.

Over time, you should try to become someone who makes a difference in other people's lives as you grow and evolve in your industry. Many times something happens in a day, and you smile to yourself and think, "That's what CH told me years ago," or, "That was the advice Mike gave me long ago." Insert your name into these sentences, and others will remember you forever. Twice a year I get a call from a guy named Gordon. Gordon calls me on my birthday and then some day in the summer. Each year, on those days he calls me and thanks me for hiring him in what was a stretch (unconventional) hire. I made an impact on his life, and he is grateful for it. That makes me feel good, and I know Gordon will pay it forward with the people he coaches, counsels, and mentors.

During the first week in a new role, I met Mike in his office, and he held out his hand. As I looked him in the eye, I shook his hand.

He held out his hand again and said, "Empty your pockets." He took all my change, put it in his desk, and said, "I never want you to have change in your pockets again." I never have. Change is loud, and it rattles. When people are nervous, they jingle their change, and more often than not they don't even know they are doing it. Rattling change during a first impression is not positive. It prompts the other person to think, "Why are you nervous? I'm not listening to you—I'm listening to you rattling your change." The change example is a tactical point that you might not think about or realize that it matters. Details do make a difference to a client or a prospect. When you are selling, don't let little things derail you. Get rid of your change. That is one end of the barbell: a practical tactical suggestion.

Mike also provided some awesome strategic lessons for me. One in particular may help you as you go to sell stuff. I always want to be number one. I want to win and be recognized as a winner. I don't care what we play for; if we are playing for a box of pencils when you sell the most stuff this quarter, I want that box of pencils. So do you, right? I thought so. Each of us wants to be on the top of the rankings. It's not necessarily how much money, it is how you stack against your colleagues and peers.

Regarding the big picture, Mike had to have a heart-to-heart with me because I wanted to win so badly that I would crush everyone in my path. I was not a team player. When we had a sit-down, I was completely stunned. I had absolutely no self-awareness and let the blinders of my desire to win hurt me.

This is important. I don't care what you sell, there are a lot of people who help you get the sale. If you are not a team player up and down the chain, you may sell a lot of things in the short term, but you will burn out the people who help you to sell.

Looking back, I wish I would have been more patient after that talk. In retrospect, I was not ready to be as patient as I needed to be. The awesome thing about the conversation was the fact that I had a relationship with Mike that took years to build. Because of that relationship, he took the time to help me. Now don't get me wrong, I didn't view it as help at the time, but twenty years later it was exactly that. His willingness to help me has aided me in my future endeavors. From a strategic perspective, understand that your success depends on others around you. In addition, the other strategic lesson is that you need to listen to the people who have an impact on your life.

As an aside, we shouldn't wish to change things in our past. We can't change these things, and so we need to learn from them. When we don't learn from our decisions or actions from the past, we repeat them, and then its shame on us.

The other major strategic learning from Mike revolves around the ripple effect. Like a chess master who thinks several moves in advance, it is critical to take your time when making important strategic decisions. People may clamor for a decision, but it is better to wait and think about the downstream ramifications rather than make a quick decision.

I am not opposed to gut instinct decisions. What I am opposed to is gut instincts that are not thought out through the future ripples. Think about the rock you throw into a stream; that rock makes a wide first ripple. As you look closely, you will see four or five more ripples behind the first. Those four or five ripples could hurt your career in the future. Every salesperson makes decisions on a constant basis. Most decisions are good, but if you reflect back on your big mistakes, they were probably because you made a quick decision and didn't think through the future ripples.

Most of the decisions that you made that turned out wrong were probably in a grey area, where you could go either way on the decision. We operate in grey areas all day long. The black-and-white decisions are easy to make. When you have an important decision that sits in a grey area, you need to allocate extra time to make the appropriate decision. The decision may not work out, but that's okay; it's when you make a snap decision and it goes wrong that you kick yourself.

It takes a team to complete a sale. If you make promises for other team members without understanding how things are developed, made, shipped, or serviced, then you may get the first sale, but you may not get the second sale because the next ripple was an inappropriate delivery date for an order. You may not get the referral, a part of your diversified sourcing strategy, with the next ripple because you promised a level of service that is either cost prohibitive or unavailable. These are simple ripple examples. I need you to think about the ripples as you make strategic decisions.

The last strategic concept I will leave you with in this section may be difficult to do. A self-aware person might consider being proactive and reaching out to her or his boss. Have a conversation about becoming a better team player. Spend the time working with your boss to help other team members do well and become better in their roles. A terrific way to ask your boss for advice is, "If you were me looking at my results, what would you have me do differently? What would you add to what I am doing to take my results to the next level?"

By asking for advice, you are actually flattering your boss by acknowledging he or she can add value and help you. Most of the time, you will get valuable feedback. Many times bosses leave people alone for fear of rocking the boat or messing up the current operational rhythm. Reach out and ask for advice.

In summary:

- The small, tactical things do make a difference.
- Don't win at all costs. Learn from my mistake, which Mike corrected early in my career.
- Understand that every decision you make has ripples that can affect everyone, including your loved ones.

## Vocabulary

Visualize: to imagine or remember someone or something by forming a picture in your mind

## Activity

1. What small tactical changes can you make to become more effective? (change analogy)
2. What action steps can you take to become a better team player? (winning-at-any-cost analogy)
3. Take time and sit back and consider the ramifications of your decisions—not just your decisions, but your process to make those decisions? (ripple analogy)

# PART 1:

## Who Are You?

# Time to Use Your Brain

Although it would be nice to give you a long list of tactical action steps to help you sell more stuff, I would be doing you a disservice. You might want to jump right into actions, but I need you to focus on another major strategic concept. I need you to focus on *contemplation*. Too often we are so stressed about the "today" of our lives we don't contemplate the "tomorrow." If you are selling something, ask yourself, "Am I totally happy?" If you answer no, or if you could be happier, the concepts of risk, patience, and taking smart chances should enter into your thinking. To start, you need to bank "think time" at least once a week. Think in private and in a quiet space. It is time for you to begin to write down your thoughts. After a few months, a thread of opportunity may present itself.

How much think time should you have? I really don't have a good answer for you. It can be different for each person. A good start would be to block thirty minutes once a week away from the chaos of your daily life. Commit to this time and consider your thirty minutes as part of the activities in this book. Nothing may happen initially, and that's okay. You need to relax, decompress, and drop all the to-dos in your brain to make your think time valuable. One key is being consistent with your think time. You can't do this once a month and hope it will work. Hope is not a strategy of any value to you.

If you choose to do nothing but work, you may pick up your head from the cube one day and wonder where all this grey hair came from. Don't let time pass and then have regrets. The job will still be there if you spend time once a week thinking. In fact, as you get comfortable thinking, the ideas you will generate will make you wish you'd lifted your head out of the cube a few years ago.

Right now I can hear a lot of you saying, "I can't commit to thirty minutes per week." Besides pointing out that "can't" means "won't," I do empathize with you. Start with fifteen minutes once a week to map out some big or little ideas, and then commit to more. The key is to be consistent and then expand the time each week. We often spend the time thinking about work but not our future. By improving ourselves, we will improve our work results.

It is uncomfortable for most of us to invest the time to think about our lives and then write down your thoughts and ideas. Great ideas can come in the blink of an eye or over a long period of time. Each of us has had great ideas that we didn't write down, and the next morning we have a tinge of regret that we had a great idea but lost it. Be prepared for your next great idea. Keep a pen and a pad of paper on your nightstand, in your purse, or in your suit jacket; jot down what strikes you as interesting.

Of course, you have to act when you decide you have an awesome idea. I had to commit to spend weekends and nights mapping out this book while I worked more than full time. Once I got rolling, it became fun to think about all the wonderful people who have helped me in life. One day you will have an awesome idea that will help you sell more, and you will be recognized and rewarded. You will have a little more fun and smile a little more. I know that it sounds too good to be true, but you know what? If you don't take the time to think, you won't have a great idea to write down or act upon!

## Vocabulary

Contemplate: to spend time considering a possible future action, or to consider one particular thing for a long time in a serious way

Patience: the ability to accept delay, suffering, or annoyance without complaining or becoming angry

**Activity**

Think about these two questions:

1. What are two things you would like to change in your life or at work? Write both down in the margins next to this box, or in a notebook to keep yourself organized.
2. Commit to blocking at least thirty minutes a week to consider actions to change those two things, or use that committed time for the other activities I will ask you to execute.

As you read the next few sections, I need you to stay with me. You may have a desire to get to actions, and that is understandable. I promise that I will give you a long list of actions, activities, and to-dos before the book is complete. The first part of the book focuses on you, who you are, and why you are special. You may think that these are soft topics, but they are not—they go to the core of developing relationships. The main driver of more sales is stronger relationships, and that starts with a clear understanding of who you are and what value you can personally deliver to clients and prospects.

# What Are You Selling?

I would suggest that a key to selling is *understanding* who you are and what is special about you. People who sell a lot are very comfortable with the person they see in the mirror. We are not perfect, but we know who we are. We know our strengths and our gaps. We are not afraid to share either our strengths or opportunities with people. We strive to get better and in turn help others who also want to get better.

That openness about who you are helps you to establish a relationship that is not about the next *transaction*, but a long-term commitment that benefits your prospects, your company, and eventually you.

Here is a terrific group exercise that works with five to fifteen of your colleagues; the following section about Frank is the end product of this exercise. The exercise is called "What makes you special?" Trust yourself with this exercise and just go with it.

Everyone in the group takes out a piece of paper and writes his or her name at the top. All the blank papers are handed to a moderator. The moderator passes each page in random, one per person. The moderator says to start, and you look at the name on the paper. You have 90–120 seconds to write one or two comments about that person: what you admire about her or him or what makes her or him special. Write what pops into your mind, not what you think is politically correct or what people will be pleased to read.

Do not read other comments. When the moderator says time, pass to the left. When you get your page, don't read anything—just pass to the left when time is called. At the end the moderator passes the papers out to each individual. You may choose to share what you learned, what commonality arose, and what hit home to your heart (not your mind). The heart part is important because you develop relationships with your heart, not your head. The point is simple: you are special.

You need a solid grasp of what is special about you in order to create an emotional and intellectual foundation upon which to build. So, what makes you special? Who are you? Now is the time to take the data from the group exercise and block time to write down what makes you special. You need to do this because later on I am going to ask you to convey this to clients and prospects.

What do you do? Write down what you sell or what you want to influence.

Why do you do what you do? Write down what drives you, gets you excited, and puts a smile on your face when you get out of bed. Think about the path you took to get to the point where you are right now. That path led you to why you are doing what you do today, and there are some very interesting twists and turns in the path you should write down.

Why should a prospect work with you? Write down what you offer, what your company offers, and what your team offers.

What can you do for your prospects? Write down how you will help them to achieve their vision, how you will provide options, and how you will help them grow (however they classify growth). Write down real stories of your achievements and accomplishments in helping other people. Writing down why you are special allows you to frame out how you approach people to share your story.

It does not matter what you are selling—you are sharing who you are. Who you are is a fundamental building block to your foundation of a strong, lasting relationship.

What you are selling is not a product, a service, or an idea. What you are selling is you. You need to be prepared to share how special you are in a genuine manner.

## Vocabulary

Understanding: something that you have reason to believe

Transact: to do business, to buy or sell things; transaction

### Activity

1. Look back and write down the answers to the questions I just posed to you. It may take you more than thirty minutes to do so, but please commit the time to do this.
2. Many people will not take on the personal risk to execute on the exercise of "what makes you special," but the people who do will be rewarded. I would ask you to gather a small group of peers and friends and do this exercise in the next two weeks, if possible.

# Case Study: Frank—With Passion

In the last section, I asked you to execute the group activity called "What makes you special?" I did this exercise with a group of fifteen leaders in Southern California, and they viewed it a bit skeptically at first. By the end of the session, people were genuinely touched by what other people wrote about them. The leaders left the meeting with a piece of paper that they will keep forever, memorializing why their peers think they are special. That piece of paper will also help them when they are at low points; they can pull it out and put a smile on their face when they read all the positive things people said about them.

I also wanted to highlight a leader who was not in the room. I selected a leader who was executing on all the critical few objectives of his company and used this person, Frank, as the case study of a well-rounded leader.

I specifically selected Frank for this group. Frank is a leader with *passion*. Frank believes to his core that what he does and what his firm does is the absolute best in the industry. When you meet Frank, he has passion and determination to make sure a prospect truly understands how great it would be to work with Frank and use the products and services he can provide. This passion cannot be faked; it is genuine. Although we may not show our passion and belief like Frank, if we want to sell more, we must believe we can help others.

Here are the characteristics that the group discussed about Frank. I bring these up because I will ask you to reflect on Frank as you reflect about yourself.

- He smiles a lot and makes other people feel good. It is so easy to smile. Why do we let things get us down? Then our face hurts from all the negative energy generated by frowning.

- He appreciates the situation he is in and gives thanks for the opportunity. When Frank gives thanks, he thanks the entire team, the corporate team, the external partners who helped get to yes, and anyone who touched the sales process. Even when the job is tough and it is a bad week, he remembers how lucky he is to have the opportunity to help people while making a significant amount of money. Sometimes we get so caught up in the daily nonsense that we don't take a step back to be thankful that we have a job. We need to be a little more thankful because there are a lot of people who would love to be in our shoes right now.

- Frank is an *optimist*. Whereas everyone gets down or goes through poor sales cycles, Frank believes things will turn around with his hard work.

- He is genuinely interested in his clients and prospects. At a recent lunch Frank exhibited that he has actively listened at past meetings. He asked multiple open-probe questions about the prospect's family and stayed away from business until the end of the lunch, where he positioned a sale by year end. Frank also positioned the next meeting two weeks out and the proposed agenda, which included providing answers to some of the prospect's objections.

- He is *patient*. Frank has had sales cycles that run ninety days to five years. The beauty of Frank's prospect pipe is that he knows everyone in his territory. He doesn't always know when the next sale will happen, but Frank usually gets a chance to get the sale.

- He doesn't always win; Frank loses more than he wins. That's okay because he plays in so much more traffic than the average person. He is disappointed when he loses, but he keeps prospecting. And when he loses, he keeps in touch with the prospect because one never knows when a purchase or move was a mistake. Staying in touch allows Frank to get back in the game.

- He gives away credit. At a recent client and prospect event, Frank gave all the credit away to his team for pulling off the event. He acted as if he did nothing and was just along for the ride, despite the fact that he was prepared and was the keynote speaker. I was riding up the elevator to Frank's office with a client who dropped off a $1.4 million check and was praising the event. Give the credit away, and it will come back to you tenfold.

- He is relentless in the chase. Frank is the bulldog with his jaws clamped to the back of a car bumper. Frank does not give up. It may take five years, but everyone will eventually work with Frank.

In that peer-to-peer group session, here are the traits that other people see in Frank: consistent, on his game, runs through walls, personal, has your back, relentless, confident, passionate, believable, organized, authentic, competitive, knowledgeable.

A by-product of the exercise with Frank was unexpected. One of the Southern California leaders took a photograph of the "Frank list" and sent it to him. Frank, unknown to us, was in a slump. He sent back the nicest note of thanks to the team. I left the meeting feeling great because I had impacted a large group of people who would remember that day for the rest of their careers. Frank felt great that people thought so highly of him. The team felt great because they had a list of positive traits that others thought of them. All of this was accomplished when the team agreed to open up, take on some personal risk, and get out of their normal corporate comfort zone.

## Vocabulary

Passion: a powerful emotion or its expression

Optimism: the tendency to be hopeful and to emphasize or think of the good part in a situation rather than the bad part, or the feeling that in the future good things are more likely to happen than bad things

Patience: the ability to accept delay, suffering, or annoyance without complaining or becoming angry

## Activity

1. Go over the characteristics of the Frank list; circle what you want to work on and star where you are already awesome.
2. Compare your list of stars with the list of questions you answered in part one of the last activity. Rewrite your work if you missed things where you are special.

# Why You Work

You are currently working in a role because it meets up to three main needs. The first need is being fairly compensated. The second need is job satisfaction and having a little fun with your job. The third need is your personal growth and development. Ideally you would like to meet all three needs. In reality, you are happy if you meet two needs. Let's do a quick overview of the three needs and see how satisfied you are in your current role.

## 1. The first area revolves around being *fairly* compensated.

This doesn't mean you are making what you would like to make. It means you are okay making what you make based on your efforts. The most successful salespeople always feel underpaid. Even when you receive a monster check, there is still something in the back of your mind that says, "I probably should have made a little more."

The word "fairly" means different things to different people. Your boss may believe the compensation you make is fair. You, on the other hand, may have a broader view of the external environment and see how other people are compensated. You are not too interested in what other people make in your company, but in how much you make. Meeting in a place between you and your boss is where the word "fair" fits. Neither of you are perfectly happy, but you both agree that what you are paid is fair.

Even when you feel you're fairly compensated, compensation has a few pitfalls. In order to ensure that you continually meet this need in your present job, consider the following points as you are having success:

- Most firms begin to cut territories when high-performance salespeople start breaking the bank. Be prepared to fight for the territory that you believe can maximize your income as well as the company's.

- You should expect your company to raise your goals each year; this goes with most sales roles. If the goals are unachievable, you need to have the conversation with the decision makers. Unreasonable goals are a way of lowering your rate. Don't let the optics of a compensation plan fool you. By optics I mean the visual appeal of a price, plan, or deal that seems too good to be true. If the rate you get paid is appealing but your goals are not achievable, the optics won't matter because you will not obtain your sales goals.

- The converse is that there is an expectation that if you hit the home run, you are paid like the all-star. You want to be at a firm that has no problem paying the large compensation check if you get outsized results. Great firms embrace the concept of uncapped compensation for their salespeople because every dollar above goal increases their profit margin.

- A disconnect can happen when finance or HR thinks they can do your job, and so they increase your goals and reduce your rate. That is not a good combination. Those same people think they can do the job when they are tucked away in their beds reading a book, and you are on your third late-night dinner or second flight of the week. You have to be very careful with this combination: don't overreact, and attempt to alter the plan.

- As you have success, be very careful when a firm wants to spread the wealth. I am not a fan of wealth redistribution. If you work for it and earn it, then you should keep it. There will always be a fifth quintile. The low-activity, low-effectiveness people should not share in your sweat equity.

Safety Tip: Never let the boss know you are happy with your compensation. When you do, your targets go up and your basis points/commissions/rate will go down!

Safety Tip: When a new compensation plan proposal is unveiled that may appear negative, don't jump through the phone line. Count to ten and then seek to understand using fact-based feedback on the realities of the job.

## 2. The second area that keeps you satisfied in your job is that you are having some fun.

When you have fun in your current role, you can brush off some of the minutiae and focus on what's important to you: your team and your family. Great firms find ways to motivate top producers not only with compensation but with job satisfaction and a little fun in the role.

Fun can be defined many different ways. You may participate in trips with your spouse, friend, or significant other. You do not win those trips, but you earn those trips. The recognition you receive makes you feel great and allows you to be with similar top producers around the country. Maybe you have a charity that is special to your heart; many companies allow you to work within the community as a volunteer, or they provide a matching contribution. Helping your community and community involvement provides valuable *intrinsic* meaning.

Fun doesn't have to be recreational. Fun can be idea sharing what's working or not working in order to pick up ideas on how to be more efficient. It can be helping someone who needs an extra nudge, and you become a mentor. Fun can be sharing the latest news on a competitor to help everyone sell more.

Everyone has a different view of what fun is. If you haven't taken a step back to consider what fun is for you, you might want to think about that. When you have more fun, you sell more.

### 3. The third area that provides job satisfaction is when you see yourself growing and developing.

I always value it when people invest in me to help me be more productive, to expand my personal skill sets, or to give me stretch goals. Personal growth and career development is part of every human resources manual. Rarely does a company execute on it. The company that has the foresight to invest in external resources like a coach or mentor is the company that truly values its employees.

Group events at corporate are nice for networking and idea sharing, but the company that decks specific resources to a core of top performers is a company with whom you want to associate. Too often, though, when the sector turns down, they pull back on that investment. This is exactly when they should double down on that investment—not with more people, but with the same people. If you are a leader in a company and have identified your first quintile performers, now is the time to make sure there are *tangible* career-development resources invested.

At first your star performers will grumble that it is time away from sales or time away from what's important to them. Once they get into a personal development session that is well organized and thought out, they begin to rethink the "this is a waste of my time" feeling.

In these sessions:

- They participate with people who produce the same or better results
- They idea exchange on what's working
- They learn how to solve for gaps or objections from other people who have faced them and found a solution
- They appreciate being recognized by senior leadership

- They have their views heard and considered
- They build deeper ties to others in the company as well as the company itself

One of the most valuable gifts given to me was by a guy named Mike whom we just discussed. He grouped me with nineteen other people throughout a large firm, and we had an opportunity to work with an external coach. An external coach can provide a fresh perspective and ask the questions that need to be asked in a safe and nonthreatening environment. I have a lot of gaps, and one of those gaps was patience. Well, I can't really say "was" because things never happen fast enough, but I am aware of this gap and work at it. I encourage you to work in the coaching conversation at your midyear or year-end review. Get commitment from your firm to invest in a coach for you.

If you have all three of the satisfaction drivers, then you are in a very special place. Most people stay in the role if they have two of the three. If you have one of the three, you likely won't be in the role long term and are probably already looking for a new job.

If you run a company, keep an eye on these three topics with your best people. I'm concerned about the three topics for the people who drive the majority of your sales.

## Vocabulary

Fairly: in a way that is right or reasonable and treats people equally

Intrinsic: basic to a thing, being an important part of making it what it is

## Activity

1. Please rate your satisfaction on the three needs for job satisfaction, where ten is the highest satisfaction and zero is the least.
2. Spend some time thinking about how you can increase your numbers. You may not be in the perfect job, but I want you to be happier. Happier people sell more.

# Your Elevator Pitch

Let's move away from the job satisfaction topic and into a deeper review that revolves around you personally. I need you to do a deeper self-assessment and then create your personal value proposition or elevator pitch.

My daughter Meghan was home on a break from college, and we were discussing this book. Meghan asked me, "Are you going to talk about an elevator pitch?" Although I said yes, I forgot that I must have mentioned the concept to her and her brothers, John and Thomas, at one time or another.

Our objective in this section is to begin to form a narrative to which other people can relate. This is a reflection of who you are and why you are special. Each of us brings different, awesome attributes and life experiences that are special and can make the lives of others better. Call this brief narrative your elevator pitch. The elevator pitch is something you have heard of. Unfortunately, it is something that people don't take seriously, don't take advantage of, or don't put enough effort into perfecting. There are three main reasons the elevator pitch falls short.

1. Lack of preparation
2. Lack of a commitment to the concept
3. Personal insecurity

Many concepts in this book require preparation. As we work hard, the days turn into weeks, and we don't execute on the commitments we made to ourselves. Practice does make perfect with your personal elevator pitch.

Let's map out a way to create your elevator pitch.

- Define who you are. Spend time writing down who you are. Take a look at your resume, and take a look at what your social media presence says on LinkedIn. Then, review the bullet points for your earlier work.

   "I have been in the software industry for more than twenty years helping my clients increase productivity while expanding margins. The work is rewarding, and we have become really involved with the community and our clients' charitable organizations. It has been rewarding to be involved locally while also helping our clients' businesses grow. At this point in my career, with the kids in college, I always enjoy developing new connections."

   The math may not work out perfectly, so prepare thirty seconds of content. When you start writing things down, let all your thoughts, emotions, feelings, and memories pour out. All that content is worth its weight in gold and will help you to become more effective in developing relationships and thus selling more stuff.

- Explain what you do. Spend time writing down what you do. Look back at past jobs in your industry as well as what you currently do. Think about the lessons you have learned in your journey and how they have helped other people.

   "As our industry has evolved, I have found that our cloud solution is differentiated from the competitors in several key areas. Our solution is just the start of the relationship; with our company we have many ways to leverage your firm's productivity in a cost-efficient manner."

- Spend time describing why you do what you do. Think along the lines of what is important to you, what is important to your company, and, most importantly, what is important to the client or prospect.

  "As time has passed, I get so excited with new innovations that we have pioneered in the health-care sector that help my clients. We work in partnership to execute on specific, individual objectives, and as we achieve them, we celebrate our success together. It's a great feeling to put my head on the pillow each night and be pleased with helping people in such a difficult and competitive business environment."

- Characterize what you can bring to the table, and ask for a potential meeting. Spend time writing down what you can contribute. Again, reflect on past work and personal experiences where you have helped others. The focus is on you, but the end objective is to get a meeting to sell more. You need to always keep the client or prospect in your line of focus.

  "The experience I have tied to our solution set has helped my clients increase their productivity by 20 percent. If we can block some time for a cup of coffee next week, I can share with you the key drivers to that productivity increase that could occur for you."

Safety Tip: "ABC" stands for "Always Be Closing." Too often we deliver an awesome elevator pitch, and then nothing happens because we don't ask for something.

If you are having a hard time getting this section crisp, here are some questions that can help form your elevator pitch. If you answer each one, you don't have an elevator pitch but a book! On your first pass, that's okay. I would prefer too much content that can be edited versus really important content that you forgot to include.

Do a brain dump on these questions: Where did you grow up? Where did you go to school? Have you moved? How did you get into the industry? What's unique about your family? What special interests or charities do you support? What do you do for fun? What's your biggest impact on a person? What are you most proud of? Who has had the largest impact on you personally and professionally? What was a big gap that you fixed? What do you like sharing with people about yourself? What else can you think about that is special and unique?

Once you have worked through these segments, it is time to practice. You can now spend some time in front of your mirror piecing the main components of your elevator pitch together and timing yourself.

## Demonstrate, Observe, and Perfect

### Demonstrate

Practicing or role playing with peers is very difficult. You expose your weaknesses to colleagues, and that can lead to a feeling of *vulnerability*. You need to get over that fear of vulnerability. See into the future, and see how awesome it is to flawlessly execute your elevator pitch to a room full of well-paying prospects. Practice with someone like a colleague.

### Observe

Observe others telling their story. In this instance you need to employ active listening. You may like how they tell their story, how they structure their stories, or how they deliver their stories. If it works, use it yourself. Please don't have so much pride that you won't use what works for other people. It may not work for you word for word, but you may be able to tailor it to your personal style.

## *Perfect*

*Perfect* your elevator pitch with your peers and then have some fun delivering it. You need to be slow and comfortable telling your story. Imagine getting hit by a bus. (Just a graphic example—please do not try this at home!) After getting hit by the bus, you stand up and are so comfortable with your story that you pick up where you left off. There was a time when I had to deliver a major presentation. I remember practicing that speech a hundred times while walking on a beach. I truly felt like I would stand up after the bus hit me and not skip a beat. That's the *commitment* you need to make to your elevator pitch.

Your elevator pitch must be genuine, practiced, and from your heart.

## Vocabulary

Vulnerable: able to be easily hurt, influenced, or attacked

Perfect: complete and right in every way; having nothing wrong

Commitment: a promise to give yourself, your money, your time, etc., to support or buy something

## Activity

1. I trust by now you know exactly what I am going to ask you to do. I have a personal opinion that your desire to improve means nothing if you don't act on your commitments. I am asking you to start to write down your personal elevator pitch.
2. "I am in the process of expanding my business. To do that, I really want to hone my personal—not our company—my personal story. When you think about me, what do think about?"

Present this narrative to your top ten clients and you will probably receive similar thought threads that you can weave together with future prospects.

# Accountability Partners

Who keeps you honest? I believe one person should be your *accountability* partner, or AP. An AP is a person whom you talk with and share your activity, frustrations, and challenges. This is the person with whom you demonstrate, observe, and perfect. This is a person who knows you but doesn't necessarily have to be your best friend. Many future activities in this book ask you to leverage your accountability partner, so spend time thinking about the topic before you engage someone to be your AP.

Your accountability partner should be someone:

- Whose opinion you value
- Who is willing to help you with no expectation of a return
- Who will listen to what you have to say
- Who will not judge you
- Who won't use you to better his or her own position
- Who will be brutally honest with you

In turn, you must not be offended by feedback. Many times we walk down the correct path, where we seek advice, guidance, or coaching—but when we receive it, we don't like it. There is personal risk when you decide to embrace the concept of an accountability partner. You first have to drop the inclination to say what you think the AP wants to hear and not what you actually believe. You then have to embrace the fact that an AP will make you personally uncomfortable along your journey together.

Not putting in the effort with an AP is like the high-activity, low-effectiveness person. The blame game is easy. People forget the opportunities they had if they would have made the time and invested in an AP. The effort is a two-way street: if your AP doesn't believe you are putting in the effort and are using him or her as a "check the box" for the boss, then the relationships falters quickly.

How do you structure an AP relationship? Very carefully! Let's look at two methods.

## I. Group share or group study

A group of like-minded leaders gathers for a thirty-minute phone call, scheduled at the same time and day each week, for an entire year. The objective is to share best practices, document the ideas, and share with the group in soft copy. Groups like this are made of leaders across geographic territories. This helps to bring fresh thinking and new ideas from different parts of the country, where prospects may respond in new or different ways. The ideal group size needs to be manageable and must allow participation by all members. Attempt to keep the group between six and nine members.

Sometimes the ideas shared are basic.

- The number of calls made to prospects
- The number of messages left
- The number of face-to-face meetings held
- The number of first meetings
- Reports on local competitive intelligence
- The number of offers
- The number of new personal e-mail addresses
- The number of events attended
- Results of event-driven activities

Sometimes the ideas are "ah-ha" moments that drive activity, like a focus on something of which you were unaware. Sometimes the call to action takes a developmental turn. "John, you said you were going to talk to twenty prospects on a topic last week, and you didn't. Why is that?" That silent pause ensures John will make his calls next week. Remember, personal accountability is a large function of these meetings or one-on-one discussions with your AP.

What you may find is that a group like this grows as best-practice notes get circulated and people want to dial in. Start and end on time. You don't want pretenders that talk far too much and waste the group's time. Someone needs to have a conversation in private with those people and either alter participation habits or remove them from the group. These calls are not for people who want to have their names on the list to show the boss. These calls are for people who want to change, learn, grow, and help make a difference.

## II. AP intimacy

The more intimate approach is a one-on-one AP relationship. You should use the same structure for discipline and consistency, but with two people. You tend to have deeper and more meaningful conversations with just one person. One-on-one accountability partners are perfect for role playing before you try your approach with a prospect. Prospects can be hard to come by, so practice is critical.

Embrace an accountability partner for the right reasons (explained here) and transform your results while forging a stronger relationship that will last a lifetime.

Should your accountability partner be internal or external to the company? The answer is yes. If you embrace the concept of an accountability partner, you might consider having two: one at your firm and one not affiliated with your firm.

Ideally, your internal accountability partner will be in a different geographic territory to you. I like different territories because you probably spend enough time with people in your area. Having someone in a different geography can bring fresh or different thinking; it can expose you to ideas that you may not be aware of because most companies get everyone together infrequently. Having a different geography can also be less threatening than someone in a similar territory or region.

Where possible, it is also productive to be able to bounce ideas, thoughts, or gaps with an external person not attached to the business. If you have an external partner, you may get a fresh perspective from a different industry. With an external accountability partner, you can also test new ideas or push limits for feedback before implementing them in your firm.

Internal and external accountability partners should be people whom you like and trust. As you develop relationships with your internal and external accountability partners, there will be times of friction. During those times, wipe away any anger or frustration and really try to listen and understand why someone is giving you fact-based, critical feedback. It should not be to hurt you—it is about helping you. Feedback is humbling, and there is no way around it. You should accept the humbling part as a gift.

Once your partnership is in place, you should try to touch base every week to discuss the prior week.

Ideas for Discussion:
- Did you do what you said you were going to do? If not, why?
- What are you doing to course correct so that you don't repeat a gap again?
- What did you learn the prior week?
- What was a positive surprise?
- What was a negative surprise?
- Any "ah-ha" moments?
- What are you committing to the following week?

If you had all the answers and lived in a perfect world, you wouldn't need accountability partners. I know I don't have all the answers. Commit to an AP.

## Vocabulary

Accountable: responsible for and having to explain your actions

Partner: one of two people who do something together or are closely involved in some way

## Activity

1. Make a list of potential internal and external accountability partners during the next seven days.
2. Over the next two weeks, explain the concept of an accountability partner to your top three prospects. When you find the right person who will commit to help you, start by sharing your elevator pitch.

# Case Study: James—Against the Odds

James was one of the first leaders who embraced the concept of an accountability partner. He and his accountability partner, Gene, worked well together and helped each other. I get a smile on my face every time I think about James. He is an awesome sales leader who has been through a lot. James has a heavy accent, and at one point his boss wanted to move him to a new job because he thought people couldn't understand him. James was producing middle-of-the-road results, not first quintile results. James got to a point where he knew he had to change things up or wallow in mediocrity.

Instead of giving up, James doubled his efforts and became a star salesperson. Don't skip forward just because you don't have the issue James faced; that is not the point of this chapter. Everyone knows people who have beaten long odds or negative odds, as well as people who have not beaten long odds. What's the difference between those people?

James made a conscious decision to change. These are very *facile* words, and I understand that. Please understand that the simplest concepts can lead to the greatest transformational changes. You don't need an incomprehensible concept to make a big change; the biggest changes come from the simplest concepts to which you commit.

I want to say each and every one of you reading this book has something to work on. I know I have to work on things. Let's discuss what James did to change things and become a success.

1. He asked for help by enrolling an accountability partner. Asking for help is a sign of strength, not a sign of weakness. A really strong leader named Pat urges people to ask for help because he does not want to leave any person behind. Don't struggle quietly with the world on your shoulders; ask for help and leverage the world's knowledge. What is interesting about James is that he committed to an accountability partner and then held meetings every week. Too often we commit to something and then let it fade when things are working out.

2. James swallowed his pride and gave up thinking that he could do everything himself. He matched his skills with someone who had skills that would help. He became more effective with his activity. Don't give in to your pride. Admit that you need some help from the person in the mirror, and then look out the window and find the help. James found Gene, and they still speak weekly.

3. He refused to quit. James could have given up, and no one would have blamed him. It is so darn easy to quit and move on. That's why some people are average: they take the easy route, quit, and find something else to do. Once you quit one thing, it can become an easy habit to keep quitting other things. That is a *vicious,* negative *cycle* that isn't fair to you or your family.

   James improved himself by joining a center of influence group. Centers of influence are people and organizations that may not directly help you sell more but that provide contacts and connections that could lead to more sales in the future. James joined a COI group that focused on public speaking. James practiced his sales approach with a group of professionals on a weekly basis. That practice made James a better public speaker in style and substance. Along the way, he made new connections and relationships that helped him earn new clients and prospects.

That practice also awakened in his peers the fact that James was working harder than them and was earning more new prospects. This was despite the fact that his peers didn't have the gaps James had. That realization helped create competition and personal accountability with peers.

4. He worked with an accountability partner and practiced his personal and corporate value proposition. A funny thing happens when you practice.

   o Everyone learns and picks up sales pointers
   o You pick up on new best practices
   o You learn suggestions to overcome objections
   o You have some fun along the way

James made the decision to have a positive attitude instead of lamenting his lack of success. He didn't give in to the personal doubts that lingered in the subconscious. He didn't give in to an easier job that would have made his life easier but in the long run would not been beneficial to his family. Once James doubled down on his effort and rebuffed any thought of quitting, he built a quality pipe of prospects that will pay off for years to come.

Was that easy? Not all the time. Was it fun? Not at the start. James did start having some fun once he had some success. When you start having little wins, you smile more, keep the effort level up, and are willing to stay at the office longer because you know your next little win is just minutes away.

A terrific intended consequence also happened: his prospects turned into clients who now regularly refer similar or larger prospects to him. James invested in an awesome sales experience because he truly cared about his prospects who became clients. Once his prospects were clients, they saw he was genuine and did not drop them after the sale. James now has his clients selling for him; they shared their personal experience, and the referrals flow. The clients didn't know they were selling for James because they were simply sharing a fact-based experience. That leverage is priceless because a warm lead that has a happy friend is much easier to close.

When you reflect on very successful people, they tend to leverage other people to help get to yes. Successful people like James also realize that asking for help is not a sign of weakness but a sign of strength.

Change the little things, and you move up the rankings. Sell more and take care of your loved ones.

## Vocabulary

Facile: easy or too easy; not needing effort

Vicious circle: a situation in which one problem causes another one, making the original problem impossible to solve

## Activity

I would now ask you to do a few things:

- Identify what is not working and write the items down
- Decide if you are going to address what's not working; simply write yes or no next to each item
- Leverage your accountability partner if you wrote that you wish to improve

# PART 2:

Building Relationships

# Selling vs. Building Relationships

A key premise of this book is that you can't sell as much as you want unless you develop a genuine relationship with your clients or prospects. In the first part of the book, we explored you and how special you are, and we began to package that for clients and prospects.

In this next section I am going to provide a framework to help you develop relationships so that your clients and prospects understand your genuine desire to help them. In our desire to sell more right now, we are probably losing more sales than we are earning if the focus is constantly ringing the cash register, trying to maximize earnings in the short term, or dumping product off the shelves to increase our receivables. Instead of trying to sell more right now, consider truly understanding the needs of your clients or prospects today.

To do that, you need to develop relationships. If you take nothing away from this book other than "develop relationships," you will have quantum growth. You can't just say, "Hi, I'm John. I'd like to develop a relationship with you!" That's not realistic or genuine, and it does not have a shred of integrity in the approach. You have to understand the value of building relationships and then invest the time to develop those relationships.

You also need *scale* to sell. That means you need clients whom you have a relationship with and who will buy more from you over time. Even if you are selling ideas or transformational change, the people helping to make those decisions won't be sold unless there is a meaningful connection that is fostered through a strong relationship.

As you read this book, you will recognize concepts that relate to scale. Scale allows you to have a repeatable process that can turn into a referral machine. It is so much easier to sell a lot more stuff when you have people advocating on your behalf. That's what scale delivers.

I may not be right 100 percent of the time. You may make a onetime sale and keep everyone happy in the short term. The problem is that if the initial sales don't become repeat sales, you are a gerbil in the wheel, constantly looking for your next prospect. You keep starting the year at zero and run in that wheel without a chance to think about a better way to operate. That is not scale; that is not fun.

I have seen countless people have an awesome first year in sales, and they became the toast of the company as a rising star. Unfortunately, many of these people do not repeat the following year. In hindsight, they would have been better off accepting their success and building a platform for repeatable success. A strong leader named Bill once told me no on an invitation for one of his leaders to speak at a conference after a really good first year. His reason was that he wanted to make sure the leader repeated her success before providing exposure that might become detrimental to her career.

The same thing happened to me after I accepted a new role at a firm. I was asked to speak at a national conference, and the national sales manager at the time said it was too early. Greg was correct in making me wait. Besides working on patience, Greg knew that exposure too soon may not be good for my long-term career. If you are new in a sales role, consider keeping year-one success to yourself and build the process to repeat in future years. Successful leaders create leverage and scale by initiating, developing, and expanding relationships. By doing this, they reach their end goal faster, more efficiently, with less hassle, and most times with a greater sense of personal accomplishment.

The awesome end product of relationship building is that your clients and prospects see how happy you are, and they end up buying more from you. Clients and prospects want to be associated with positive, optimistic, fun people. This attitude can't be faked—it has to be genuine. As you contemplate your current situation, you may realize that you are not as happy as you would like to be. Maybe you are not as optimistic as you like. I have been through personal peaks and valleys of optimism and happiness. I can't be optimistic twenty-four hours per day, three hundred sixty-five days per year. What you can do is what I do: attempt to recognize when things are not right, and take extra time when you communicate things. By taking that time, you may not let a bad day turn into a loss of a sale or the loss of an opportunity to develop a new relationship.

As you build relationships, you create formal and informal networks that help you today and, more importantly, years down the road. These new clients become advocates and champions of the people in your network. You will realize that a one-way relationship ends up on a dead-end road where you don't have enough space to turn the car around. You are stuck, and it's no fun to be stuck because you took a shortcut or made the short-term sale that led to a dead end. Sellers end up burning contacts and wasting resources. They may get the short-term fix of a sale, but if they are the only beneficiary, then the next time they want to establish or expand a relationship, they get nowhere. The unseen but ever present network sends messages quickly and efficiently: "Don't buy from that guy—he's only in it for the quick sale, and he doesn't care about you."

Commit to building relationships.

## Vocabulary

Scale: to increase something in size, amount, or production

Relationship: the way in which things are connected or work together: a relationship is the way two or more people are connected, or the way they behave toward each other

## Activity

I have one topic I would like you to think about before we dig deep into a process that will help you develop stronger relationships.

The question you need to answer is a difficult one. When you start your day, do you think about your personal success, or do you think about the success of others? We tend to have a tendency to think about our personal success too often, and we fail to think about our prospects, peers, and colleagues. Begin to focus on others on a daily basis.

# Do the F ... O ... R ... D

I will show you a fun and easy way to think about developing relationships. In the spirit of keeping it simple, let us explore a way to learn about people.

Building relationships takes time and also requires a lot of digging and learning about the person with whom you want to spend time. A rock star leader I know broke down the relationship-building process into a few segments that appeal to all the key areas of a person's life. When I spoke to him about the approach, the first thing he said was that this content was inspired by his dad. His dad spent time with his son, helping him to understand that although developing relationships takes time, one can concentrate on key segments that can lead to stronger relationships. That was an awesome lesson!

Before we move on, let's pause and put down the book. Pick up your phone and give someone a call who has helped you to become who you are. Make someone else feel great that they are appreciated and recognized. That will be your good deed of the day.

The framework we are about to explore may help to build a foundation that leads to more sales. You will not get results with the view of, "Okay, box three is checked off, now I have a relationship and I will sell more." You need to spend meaningful, authentic time with a client or prospect to expand or establish a relationship.

The framework I am about to explain explores four key areas of a client's or prospect's life: their family, their organization, their recreation, and what their long-term dreams are. Each category allows you to learn more about very real and very important aspects of a person's life.

You have to choose to make time to build a relationship the right way. Shortcuts will not work in the long term. The person in the mirror must choose to invest the time.

In the spirit of keeping it simple, think about building relationships around four key segments. These are the four key segments.

- **Family**—Learn about their family and their family history. Family is usually closest to the heart, so it is a good investment of your time. Birthdays, anniversaries, and key dates are important to know and to keep track of. It may take time to learn about the family part from a prospect, but it usually ends up being a very meaningful part of your relationship. "You mentioned you have a sister in Minnesota. How did she end up there?" Some people do not want you to probe into their personal lives, especially at the start of a relationship. Be sensitive to any pushback when discussing personal information. Over time it has been my experience that as you share things about yourself, people will share things about themselves.

- **Organization**—Learn about their history at their current organization as well as other firms where they worked. This is also the time to see where they went to school and what their focus has been since graduating. I have found that these probes are the easiest part of the conversation to have. You may want to start with this area because it can lead to discussing the other aspects of the conversation.

  A best practice would be to view a person's professional LinkedIn profile. By looking at LinkedIn, you can start the conversation with, "Joe, you started out at your company in the Leadership Development Program, and in a few short

years have been promoted often. Tell me about your journey."
You can also learn how they got to into their current industry
and how they ended up at their current company. "Steve, you
had a long career at Nike, and now you are leading a large part
of the company. How did this happen?"

- **Recreation**—Learn what people do for fun. Finding out
what is important to them outside of work is usually more
important than what you learn about their current work. This
is an opportunity to see what organizations they belong to
and what charitable boards and groups they have a passion
for. Get your prospects talking about what gets them excited
on the weekend, or about special events in which they like to
participate.

  Recreation can be an easy conversation starter when you
have clients on the phone or face-to-face. "Meghan, tell me
about your volunteer work at Vital Voices," or "Matt, you just
finished your second full triathlon at a Rev3 event. Tell me
about it." When you discuss after-work activities or weekend
activities, you get people excited. You connect at a more
personal, not professional level.

- **Dreams**—Learn about someone's long-term dreams and
aspirations. Dreams can be the most intense part of your
conversations; these tend to be very personal and *intrinsic*
to the client or prospect. You don't start a conversation with,
"Tell me about your dreams." Over time you can begin to
probe deeper. "Thomas, your ability to connect with people
is a special gift. How does that gift play into what you are
thinking about your future?"

Take your time as you delve into dreams and aspirations. They
are very personal, and you really need to be patient as you learn about

people's dreams. Some people wear their dreams openly, but others view their dreams as deeply personal. You need to have a positive and comfortable relationship in order to discuss dreams.

One way to learn about their dreams is to share your dreams with them first. This may allow them to open up to you. "When I'm done in this industry in ten to fifteen years, I really want to go and teach at a college. I'd like to give back some of the industry and institutional knowledge I've gained over the years. What do you think about ten years down the road, Bobbie?"

By focusing on these four segments, you can easily remember where to go next as you discuss their lives. This is not an exercise where you pull out your notepad and walk down the list; it is a process that takes time and multiple meetings. I was speaking with a rock star leader recently, and he was discussing his conversion rates for a sale. He told me he met with a prospect and average of twelve times before he made the sale. His point to me was that over twelve meetings, he had gained such rich personal and professional data that he knew it was not if the prospect would work with him, but when.

## Organization

Although I repeat this a lot, you are not smart enough to remember a conversation you had with a prospect six months ago. After a meeting, go back to your car and do a brain dump on everything you've just learned. Then take those notes and put them into your easily accessible database. Some leaders pay for a service called *copy talk*. You verbally record your notes and send it to a service, and they transcribe the notes and send it back to you in written form. You can then cut and paste the notes into the section about a client or prospect, and you have everything you need for a follow-up chat. Your prospects will see that you are engaged, listen, and pay attention when you can ask them something personal like, "How did John's trip to Russia go? What did you do during your visit?" or "I know Jeremy's wife had a baby girl. How are the baby and mom doing?"

## Activity

1. Get a notecard and write down the four components of ford, one word below each other.
2. Get the card laminated and keep it in your suit jacket, purse, or someplace handy to remind yourself that you need to focus on these key areas when asking questions.

# Open Probes

It is important for you to gather information from your relationship-development process. As you begin to formulate your questions, remember to use open *probes*, not closed probes. Closed probes provide a yes or no answer and allow your prospect to end the conversation or else introduce an awkward pause.

Open probes allow your prospects to tell you what's on their mind or what's important to them. Open probes don't give them the opportunity to end the conversation before it actually starts. "Do you like your job?" is a yes/no question. The better approach would be, "Tell me, what do you like about your job?" Ask the question, and then you can sit back and listen to some compelling personal information.

Key Concept: Always ask open-ended probes that allow your clients or prospects to tell you what's important to them. Yes or no answers allow people to stop the conversation.

After each conversation, update your notes. Three months from now when you are having a conversation, you can bring up or revisit a topic you wrote about. "Did your son John get into that state department assignment?" Besides making you look smart, you show that their personal details are important to you.

Most important, the information you learn helps to form a solid foundation on which a relationship is developed. From there, you may become friends and may sell more because you know what's important to that person. Or, you may just become friends. Who doesn't enjoy a good friend?

## Vocabulary

Intrinsic: basic to a thing, being an important part of making it what it is: each human being has intrinsic dignity and worth

Probe: to search into or examine something

### Activity

Start to keep track of how many yes and no answers you get from clients or prospects. If you are asking closed probes, you need to train yourself to ask open-ended questions that allow the conversation to continue.

# Be Curious

As an extension of open probes, I want to spend a moment on curiosity. If you are *curious* about topics with your clients and prospects, then you will learn more than you ever expected. Your curiosity needs to be *genuine*; a prospect will detect a fake quickly. A great way to be curious is to ask open-ended questions and probes. This is an add-on to earlier content on developing relationships. Too often we ask yes/ no questions, and then the conversation stops, or we let a prospect dictate the next steps. Closed probes are fine if you know the answer and it's the answer you want.

Here are some open-ended probes to learn more, develop a relationship, and sell more.

- "Tell me about yourself."

   This open probe allows the prospect to take the conversation in any direction and allows you to learn about what's important to the person at that moment. Be ready for the retort, "Tell me about yourself." Share something meaningful that has impact and that is genuine. You then gain additional credibility with your client or prospect.

- "Where are you from?"

   Understanding a person's past allows you to find common ground or relate to a personal experience. You are looking for connection points that begin to develop or deepen an existing relationship. As you run into people, you can mention that, and it will be a common reference point.

- "What do you love most about what you do?" or "What do you like most about your current situation?"

  Find the passion within a person, and you will connect faster. Be ready for your brief elevator pitch about what you love about your job as well. Always be positive and learn what people believe is positive. This allows you to anticipate any objections. Tie in similarities of your firm and what they like so that they associate your firm with theirs.

- "If you could improve one thing about your current situation, what would it be?"

  Here is the opportunity to see how your product, service, or idea would benefit the prospect. Be prepared to share a solution your company implemented that fixed the same issue or avoided it for your company. This will show not only responsiveness but also problem solving that will be respected.

- "How did you get started in your business?"

  This question allows you to learn how they got into their current business and the route they took. You also learn their perspective based on what they have seen in that specific industry. As you share how long you have been in the business, try to tie in your experience with their experience so that there is a connection the prospects may reflect on at a later date. This also provides an opportunity to share common connections that you have in the industry.

- "Tell me about your business."

  This allows you to gather competitive intelligence. This

probe also allows you to formulate a game plan to learn how your prospects think about their businesses.

- "What's important to you at this stage of your career?"
  This question gets to the dreams of people. You can help to formulate recommendations to help your clients achieve their goals.

- "What is next for you?"
  It is excellent to learn how prospects think about their future and what that may mean to you. Given your personal network, you may have connections the clients can speak with to kick the tires as they think about their next move.

- "What do you admire about competitor firms?"
  This allows you to gather CI on the firms, not just their jobs. This also allows you to tie in what they like to your company, assuming there is a tie-in.

- "What groups are you a part of?"
  Looking for external connects can allow positive, warm referrals or recommendations. This is your entrance into an entirely different group of centers of influence, and it will allow you to expand your diversified sourcing strategy.

- "Tell me about your favorite client."
  Learn what type of people the prospect likes. This question allows you to begin positioning how you gather referrals as you explain what your ideal client is.

- "What are your hobbies outside of work?"
  Take the conversation away from business and begin to personalize the conversation. Given your time in the industry, you will most likely have connections to a specific hobby or

passion, and you can share a warm story that validates the importance of their hobby.

- "What is your exit strategy from work?"

  This provides short- or long-term thinking about their jobs and companies. Over time you will have the ability to share other connections that may have the experience of an exit, and you can help your prospects to think about an exit in a more effective way, thus adding value that doesn't benefit you.

- "Where will you retire?"

  Personalize the conversation and learn to where they will retire. Be prepared to provide your answer and then turn that into a positive connected statement: "You have a deal. I will visit you in Florida, and you have to promise to visit me in Bermuda!"

We all know the phrase "Curiosity killed the cat." I disagree. Curiosity helps you sell more. You take all the learned information and memorialize it in your current notes on that client or prospect. You now have a deep database of information that can be pulled up at any time to continue the conversation. You don't have the time or capacity to remember everything. Make the investment of your time to capture and save the information learned from all your open-ended probes. Be curious, my friends.

## Vocabulary

Curious: interested in learning about people or things around you

Genuine: being what something or someone appears or claims to be; real, not false

JOHN RICHARD PIERCE JR.

## Activity

I would now like to ask you two questions to think about before we continue our journey.

Have you found yourself with awkward pauses in a conversation because you asked closed-end probes? I still do it and it infuriates me. To counter the pause I rely on honesty and just say something like "Pat, I just asked a closed-end question and that was not my intent. My intent was to really understand your vision for your organization over the next three years. What are the key components of your vision?" By admitting your mistake your client or prospect will feel empathy for you and most likely keep the conversation going. Unless you want to ask a closed-end question for a purpose, I would ask you to start remembering when you used closed probes and work to improve the relationship-development process with open probes.

My second question is also simple. Do you have an organized way of learning about your clients or prospects? If the answer is no. I would encourage you adopt this with words that appeal to you in these four categories. Whenever I find myself at a dead-end conversation road I try to pivot back to one of these topics to get the other person talking.

# PART 3:

The Sales Process

# Your Target Market

I created this section because I realized too many people don't know whether they have captured the appropriate target market for their products, services, or solutions. Although you need to decide who you want to sell more to, it is not everyone. Your target market is not limitless, and so it is *imperative* that you choose wisely how you eventually approach your target market.

As you are implementing your sales process (discussed in the next section), you should take a step back and really understand the market for your products, services, or ideas. We live in a huge world, and so we have a tendency to believe our target market is just as large. It is not. The most successful salespeople—the ones who sell more, view their market with precision and focus. When you fish, you can throw a net over the side and see what you catch—potentially many different types of fish and many that may not be what you are looking for. If you know what you are fishing for, you may select a specific lure to target a specific fish and not waste your time on fish that you don't want.

A mistake some salespeople make is thinking that they have this huge target market and can do mass e-mail, snail mail, or social media, and then they'll start selling more. They take the biggest net they can find and throw it in the water. With this approach, you will definitely get in front of more people, but your materials will end up in the trash or deleted.

Using a specific lure is much different. You don't have an unlimited number of lures, so you have to prepare your approach to the specific prospect. Because your lure is for a specific fish, when you connect you tend to have more success—catching the right kind of fish or earning the right kind of new client. As you begin to identify your target market and implement a diversified sourcing strategy, you need to spend time thinking about the appropriate approach for what you are selling.

Depending on what you are selling, either approach may work. If you are selling a low-priced commodity, you need broad-based awareness of your product in order to compete. Sometimes it is okay to use a big net. Think about buying a television. How many print ads, Internet pop-ups, and advertising on the television and radio do you see and hear? The number is staggering. This market generally needs a big-net approach because the space is so competitive and the product is relatively the same unless it is at the ultra-high end of the space.

If you are seeking transformational change at your company by positioning new strategies or ideas, you need buy-in from key stakeholders, and a targeted lure approach is a must.

- Share your vision with key decision makers
- Position the benefits to people who may be hesitant at first
- Understand the ripple effects of a decision
- Get group buy-in to move forward.

Someone selling a three-hundred-thousand-dollar car has a limited target market, and a big-net approach will not work. The only approach is a targeted lure approach. That approach is typically more expensive and time consuming on the front end. On the back end, it ends up being a high-margin sale that provides significant compensation to the salesperson. If you have a mass market product with broad appeal, you may be better served with a big-net approach. Sell more TVs. If you have a more specific product or service, a tailored lure approach may be more appropriate. I can't answer your question, only you can. To do that, you need to analyze who traditionally buys your product, service, or idea, and who could potentially be a purchaser.

## Vocabulary

Imperative: extremely important or urgent

### Activity

1. Invest think time to assess your target market. Try to understand whether you are approaching the right market.
2. Test your thesis about the appropriate target market with your accountability partner.
3. Adjust your marketing approach where appropriate.

# The Sales Process

I have been spending a lot of time asking you to embrace the concept of relationship building through a better understanding of yourself. I then went deep on some tactical ways to develop relationships. What I have not focused on is the process to earn a sale from start to finish. There is danger for me in attempting to tackle such a large topic in a short book. I'm going to embrace that risk and spend some time discussing a sales process with you right now.

Before we start, let me admit a huge gap I had. I used to just wing it when it came to a sales process. I would make it up as I went along, and that led to a lot of failure. What I realized years later was that I could have been much more successful if I had been more disciplined and had thought about implementing a written, cohesive sales and prospecting process.

I can create a *plethora* of diagrams mapping out a sales process. I won't be doing that. I will walk you through some key elements of a sales process that can be modified for your purposes. Most of these concepts will be discussed later as examples by leaders who are awesome salespeople.

A key concept you have to embrace and agree with is simple: you need a sales process. You will not have sustained long-term, scalable, and repeatable sales if you are shooting from the proverbial hip. You may get lucky, but you don't want to be the guy who was the top-ranked person in one year and ranked one hundredth the next two. Some people end up number one for a year by luck or some odd coincidence, never to be heard from again. Here are the main reasons for the flame out.

- They sell out of their trunk (unorganized)
- They don't have a process (assume it will all work out)
- They don't implement a multifaceted sourcing strategy
- They believe all the good press written about them and don't work as hard

Now we get into the meat of this section with numerous concepts to build upon. These fourteen concepts can be applied across many different industries selling just about anything. I have developed them by observing professionals and through trial-and-error experience.

## 1. Identify your target market.

Understand who has historically purchased your product or service. As you think about who has purchased, focus on markets you have not expanded in and the reason you have not gone there. Early adopters are willing to test new markets without worry of failure. These early adopters to new markets tend to sell more and help map the future direction of a company.

## 2. Become well versed in your product or service.

Don't assume you know it all. You should have a working knowledge of the positives, negatives, and neutrals of your product, service, or idea. You should also have a working knowledge of what your competitors say about what you sell. By doing this you will have the ability to overcome objections (a topic discussed later). You should also know what current clients and clients that were one-time sales think about your product or service. Gather internal and external competitive intelligence on what you sell or service.

Don't just speak with the salespeople—speak with the people who manufacture, ship, invoice, package, develop, service, and troubleshoot what you sell. This "on the ground" knowledge at your fingertips will help you to learn what you need to sell more, not just the polish by your marketing department. Memorialize your learning in your database or where you keep your notes; they will become excellent memory jogs as you prospect new people.

## 3. Understand who your competitors are and identify their strategic and tactical advantages and gaps.

To whom do you lose sales? Understand who sells similar products or services and how they position their offering. Put yourself in the position of a competitor and try to find gaps in what you sell or service.

If you are selling a transformational change or a new concept, have people become devil's advocates to try to shoot holes in what you are trying to accomplish. Gather all the information and learn from it.

## 4. Understand the math of building a successful, long-term pipeline.

You may not want to hear it, but a large part of selling stuff is the math. You need to understand how many calls, how many meetings, and how many offers lead to the eventual sale. You need to understand the conversion rates between each segment as well. For example, if you want to sell four large units this year, you may need to have eight offers; that is a 50 percent conversion rate. To have eight offers, you may need to have thirty-two new meetings a year, or a 25 percent conversion rate from meetings to offers. At the front end, it may take 1,320 calls to get 32 meetings, or an approximate 2.5 percent conversion rate.

I will discuss the math at the start of the "Diversified Sourcing Strategy" section.

## 5. Map out the components of a diversified sourcing strategy.

There is an entire section in this book built around a *diversified* sourcing strategy. A diversified sourcing strategy creates a series of activities and action steps that allows you to cultivate new clients from multiple areas. This strategy allows you to grow through traditional and nontraditional ways.

The flame-out salespeople are the ones who got lucky with one element of a diversified sourcing strategy one year, and then they dropped off the face of the earth. One day you look back and say, "Whatever happened to ...?"

## 6. Leverage data entry to become more efficient.

Don't fall into the trap of "I will remember." It never happens. You need to capture and write (or type) as much information as possible. Through the sales or courting process, you can look back in an instant and have information to get to the next sale. "Jeremy, I remember after you had your first baby, your wife had some complications. How is everything today?"

CRM stands for customer relationship management. This is a formalized system to manage data and information for clients and prospects. CRM, used properly, allows you to quickly prepare for meetings, remember key facts that are important to the prospect, and provide a series of open-ended probes, as well as helps to hold you personally accountable to you activity. Without quality, fact-based, personal, and professional data that can be pulled up quickly, you will never remember the details that prove to the client or prospect that you care about them. Even if the client knows you are pulling up the data, you took the time to remember and memorialize the information. In our evaluation of why sales are not increasing, we will take a look at your CRM or customer-relationship model.

## 7. Follow Up with Prospects.

I have provided a scripted, disciplined follow-up process for the first meeting in this book. Prospect follow-up is critically important for many reasons. First, delivering on what you said you would deliver in a meeting shows that you are professional, paid attention, and are working to meet the needs of the prospect. Second, prompt follow-up leads to additional meetings and eventual sales. Follow-up on a topic also allows you to progress a stalled process. The candidates see your interest and are willing to invest more of their time with you.

It is important that you are prepared before, during, and after any client or prospect meeting. Having a script and an agenda allows you to stay on track and move toward the next meeting or sale.

The key concept here is that you need a disciplined and repeatable meeting and follow-up process. You can't have a drink and revel in a great first meeting. Without the second meeting, all you did was waste time and spend money without any results.

## 8. Subsequent Meetings (For all future meetings, follow the same process.)

There are several things to consider for the second meeting and each subsequent meeting. Some areas to consistently leverage are:

- Agenda
- Content
- Objections
- Next steps
- Follow-up
- Data entry

Leave nothing to chance as you prepare for the next meeting. The sales process may take two meetings or twenty meetings. The prospects will realize that you prepare and that you value their time. They will appreciate the investment of your time in them.

## 9. Your Presentation and Proposal.

Eventually you will get to the point where you are making a presentation and proposal to your client or prospect to sell something.

That typically does not happen in the first meeting, but it will in subsequent meetings. As you gather data and information throughout the sales process, you have the ability to prepare your presentations and proposals to meet the needs of the prospect.

I will share some best practices on presentations in section five, "Meeting with the Client or Prospect."

### 10. How you make your Offer.

The offer is the time when you are presenting your pricing, deal, or terms with the intent of closing the client and having him or her purchase what you sell.

The math part of the offer requires you to know your personal conversion rate of an offer to an acceptance, and it is very important. Knowing your conversion rate versus the most productive in your firm is more important. If you are better than the most productive, you are probably not making enough offers and thus are not doing enough front-end math. If your conversion is below the most productive person, you need to understand why and tweak what you are doing. If your conversion rate is worse than your peers, there are many things to consider: Are you prospecting the right people? Are you doing a substandard job of presenting the offer?

The art part of the offer is how you present the offer and move to acceptance. The most productive closers make the offer process a big deal and leverage as many team members as needed to get to yes.

### 11. When your client accepts your offer.

This is the very scary time for the prospect who is now a client. After saying yes, a prospect is concerned that you will then move on to the next prospect. You need to stay laser focused until and after delivery, because prospects still have many opportunities to change their minds. You need to stay close to prospects prior to delivery to keep the sale alive. There should be no early celebrating—nothing counts until the prospect takes delivery and the check clears.

Safety Tip: The most productive salespeople stay in touch with the client weekly, if not daily, until the final good or service is delivered.

Don't let the competition slip in and steal your sale. Don't let inactivity scare the prospects and have them cancel the transaction. Leverage technology: call, text, e-mail, and keep a high-touch experience going.

## 12. World-Class, Memorable Delivery

Depending on what you sell, the delivery may be quite different. If you are hiring new people on the team, you want to provide a warm and welcoming environment that makes the new team member say, "This feels awesome." If you are delivering a product, you want to ensure that the product is what clients wanted, that it works, and that the clients are satisfied. If you deliver a service, you want to ensure that the service was completed to the satisfaction of the client. Everyone sells different things, and so a memorable delivery is different for each of us. The key is to make the prospect feel very satisfied with her or his decision to become a client.

Where appropriate, gather the team that made the sale happen and celebrate with your new client. Now is the time to make your new client unbelievably pleased with her or his decision to purchase from you. You don't want a delivery experience that leaves the client saying, "That's it? Now we are done?"

## 13. How to ask for Referrals.

Referrals are the end result of a diversified sourcing strategy, allowing you to create more scale and to sell more. If you have a world-class delivery of the product, service, or idea, you can then get buy-in from the client to help other people. Referrals are warm introductions.

Although you can't avoid the dirty work of implementing a

diversified sourcing strategy, referrals can become a more important and productive part of your sales process. Referrals also tend to be a lot more fun. You get to meet new people you would not normally see over a nice glass of wine or iced tea in a relaxed environment, and your client sells for you. That's a lot easier than a cold call, right?

## 14. Restart the Process.

You now get the concept that you need to know how many new prospects you need to be in front of in order to achieve your goals based on the math. You need a viable, repeatable, scalable, and fun process to get more clients.

This was a lot of content to cover and for you to absorb. You may add aspects to this process depending on what you sell. The key take-away is that you need to have a process and be disciplined in following that process. You can't pick and choose parts that you like and then neglect others. When you do that, you stall in the process and have to start from scratch.

If you don't have a process, you are selling out of your trunk. Things get lost or get forgotten. You won't sell more stuff unless you follow your company's process, create one for yourself, and then implement every single day.

## Vocabulary

Plethora: a very large amount of something, esp. a larger amount than you need, want, or can deal with

Diversify: to become varied or different, or to make something varied or different

Process: a series of actions or events performed to make something or achieve a particular result, or a series of changes that happen naturally

## Activity

I'd like you to compare your sales process to the one outlined. If you don't have a sales process, now is the time to start. If you do have a sales process, write down any gaps you learned about in this chapter.

# Case Study: Phil—A Breath of Fresh Air

When first impressions are generated, there are three key questions that your prospect thinks about: "Do I like you? Do I trust you? Are your competent?" These are the first impression questions that are generated as you start building a relationship. Never forget that. They happen at the first meeting, and they have relevance.

- I want to work with and for people I like.
- I want to work with and for people I trust.
- I want to work with and for people who are competent in their niche.

Both clients and prospects want and need the security of an affirming answer to these three fundamental questions. The fun part of an affirmation of the three questions is that clients and prospects want to spend time with you. When they make time for you, you end up selling more, and you also feel really good about yourself. That positive self-worth is contagious and opens up a world of possibilities for you and your family.

These are three concepts upon which many people also make a quick judgment. It is important to realize that the authentic you is the best you to share all the time. Too often we tend to present what we think people want to see instead of sharing who we really are.

## Do I Like You?

At a base level we enjoy being with and associating with people we like. It's so much easier to develop a relationship with people who you like. When you like people, you tend to work better together, and you sell more together. When you like someone, you genuinely want that other person to win and will work toward that end goal. The best way to be liked is to be yourself. Don't be something you are not. Don't pretend or show a false front. If you are true to yourself, you don't have to remember how to act around Bobbie and how to act differently around Clay. You deplete too much energy and create too much stress by trying to fake out people. This is especially difficult for younger people who really want to succeed. The desire to win may make you act differently than you normally would. When that happens, you need to self-correct and go back to the authentic you, the person you look at in the mirror every morning.

"Do I like you?" is developed in the short term and the long term. You don't need to be in someone's wedding to be liked. When you are liked, people want to be with you, and that makes you feel good.

## Do I Trust You?

Becoming trusted may take more time, but people do base trust on "Do I like you?" That may not be fair, but it is true. Trust is earned over time by executing on what you said you would do. Even if the outcome is negative, if you did what you said you would and it didn't work out, you are still putting a deposit in the trust bank. The building block of trust is integrity. Without integrity, you cannot earn trust.

Once you lose a person's trust, watch out. It may take years to earn it back—if ever—and there is still a slight pause if you get it back.

Safety Tip: If you don't know an answer, be honest. Don't fake it. Don't make a short-term sale to jeopardize a relationship. Even though you may be hungry and need to put some sales on the scorecard, building and keeping trust will generate more sales compared to a short-term sale that ruins trust.

I have personally learned that giving an answer when you really don't have the right answer is a mistake. If I don't know an answer, I now instinctually say, "I don't know that answer. Let me get back to you." I'm not worried about making a mistake. I'm not worried I don't have the answer. No one has all the answers!

## Are You Competent?

You can answer that, your peers can answer that, and client surveys can answer that. Being competent doesn't mean you have all the answers. You need to have confidence in what you do, but don't exhibit hubris by faking it. The smartest people tell clients and prospects when they don't have the answer. They use this time as an opportunity to set the next meeting and go deeper on the answer the next time.

If you have skill gaps, please ask for help. There is nothing more senseless than someone who wants to win but isn't smart enough to ask for help to get better. If you have a gap, get help so that your next prospect gets a sense that you are competent.

Phil Buchanan is a friend of mine, and he is the chairman of the Cannon Financial Group, among many other meaningful endeavors. I get a smile on my face because I like Phil, and I trust him. The Phil I know today is the Phil I met years ago. Phil is authentic and real. Phil genuinely wants to get to know you. Phil also wants to help you. He is obviously competent.

If you have a chance, visit the Cannon Financial Group's website. Phil is the genesis of the three questions in this section. I believe that Phil and people like him really want to help. They add a significant amount of value to you personally as you share your brand with clients and prospects. These are the type of people upon which you should build your network, your relationship foundation.

## Vocabulary

Affirm: to state something is true, or to state your support for an idea, opinion, etc.

Cannon Financial Group: www.cannonfinancialgroup.com

## Activity

It may be helpful for you to write down examples in each area where you had positive experiences as well as negative experiences around the three questions discussed. Then you might consider reflecting on how to replicate and scale the positives, and how to minimize the negatives.

Something else for you to consider: you don't have to work with everyone just because they buy things from you. You should not sacrifice your personal ethics or standards for people you really don't like or trust. You might consider listing people who fit into this category and passing them off to someone else. You will feel better, and when you feel better, you are happier. When you are happier, you will eventually sell more.

# Quick Hits I

In this book I have created three Quick Hits sections. They are summaries of important topics revolving around the sales process, diversified sourcing strategy, and evaluating why sales are not increasing. My intent is to provide a series of brief topics and connection points to the larger themes in the book.

## Hope Is Not a Strategy

*Hope* is not a strategy. *Instinctively* you know that this comment is accurate. How many time have you personally thought, "I hope that ..."? It's okay despite what anyone will tell you. From the richest person you know to the entrepreneur sweating blood to make it work, everyone hopes it will work out. The problem is that after a while, every successful salesperson realizes that he or she won't win the lottery. In order to ensure long-term success, you need more than hope.

### Think Time

You must make the difficult commitment to take time away from the chaos of your day or week in order to think about what's working, what's not, and what can you control or help influence.

Nothing matters if you don't make time for yourself to think away from the noise of your daily life.

## Self-Evaluation

I had originally thought that it would be acceptable to say something like, "It may be completely justifiable to have an excuse or a cause for a suboptimal outcome because of someone else." Then I thought about myself and what I would really believe. I probably would have thought two words: no excuses. When we evaluate ourselves critically, sometimes we have to just admit that passing the blame or feeling better because of some third party is not acceptable. Is your performance not where you want it? No excuses.

Evaluate, in writing, what you could have done, should have done, or might have done to influence an outcome.

The person in the mirror is the person you really need to concern yourself with. A friend named Dave has an awesome mantra: "Don't look out the window—look in the mirror."

## Effort

Let us first assess whether you are giving your full effort. One way to determine that is to look at your results versus your peers. Analyze who has better results and determine what they are doing differently. Are they spending more time on core activities? Are they more effective in a particular area? This is also a productive topic to share with your accountability partner in order to understand their view of your effort.

If you are giving it your full effort, then you need to assess whether you are being as efficient as you could be in what you are doing. Can you delegate nonessential tasks? How do you rework things to have more face-to-face time in order to sell more?

Evaluate your efficiency in your effort and make tweaks to your operating model. After the tweaks, take some time to self-assess the changes and determine whether they should be edited further. Stress test with your accountability partner.

## Commitment

As someone once said, you are not "half pregnant." You need to commit to your task, to your job, and to your mission. If you don't believe in what you are doing, then you are not committed and won't be as successful as you could have been. For example, if your math says you need to dial your phone one hour per day, and you are only dialing three hours per week, you are not committed. Review the core activities in your diversified sourcing strategy; if you are only doing half of those activities, then you are not committed.

## Hope

Many tenants in this book can guide you in creating a foundation so that you don't have to hope anything works out. If you implement concepts in this book—implementing a diversified sourcing strategy, as an example, to gather more clients or prospects—you will sell more.

I'm not sure who coined the phrase "You make your own luck"— I'm sure my dad will call me up and say, "I did!"— but it is true. If you have a solid business plan to sell more, you create positive surprises throughout a business cycle. Regardless of industry, you have good cycles and poor cycles. What differentiates the star salespeople is that they seem to sell regardless of the cycle. These people don't depend on a positive cycle to feed their family; they are prepared for positive and negative times and work accordingly.

So much of selling is event-driven. If you create a foundation with clients and prospects, when an event occurs, they think of you, or you can call them. You can't cold-call someone out of the blue and trigger a sale during an event. Let me correct myself: you can, but your chance of success will be limited. If you gradually build relationships over time, something will happen, and prospects will say, "Anmol, that was the last straw. My boss just implemented these three changes, and I need to take all our conversations more seriously. Let's revisit how you can help me and my clients." That conversation does not happen on a first call. This is an example of not hoping something will work out but taking action that produces a result because of your prior effort to build a relationship.

The tactic of waiting around for your phone to ring does not work. Hoping that the phone will ring next week is not a sound business practice if you haven't done the work to generate the interest this week. When your phone rings from a client or a prospect, it is a bonus. "Jody, I'm returning your call. I appreciate the multiple voicemail messages you left me, and after looking at your LinkedIn profile, I thought it was time to have a conversation."

There are several concepts that will allow you to avoid the trap of hoping everything works out.

- As you build relationships, you create internal and external networks that provide a flow of not only competitive intelligence but new prospects who may work with you. Too often we ignore networks because we are so busy with the day-to-day. Having a network takes time and effort, but it will provide a vehicle for competitive intelligence, a referral machine, and a safety net if you have an unexpected event occur.

- As you create and refine your sales process, you will establish discipline and rigor around how you source new clients. This will help you to build a repeatable referral machine. I admit up front that it is possible to have a lucky year. That year is just that, lucky, and it probably won't be repeated. Having discipline and rigor around a process is needed for sustained success. Following a process is hard. Everyone wants to get results, and taking shortcuts may seem appealing, but they usually turn out to be bad sales, bad hires, nonrecurring sales, or in the worse sense litigation.

- As you implement a diversified sourcing strategy, you begin to mine new prospects from multifaceted areas; this allows you to close sales from areas you have not in the past. Implementing a diversified sourcing strategy will take time, effort, and a lot of work. (Do you see a theme here?)

- As you buy into the math needed to sell more and learn how to refine the art that allows you to close more, you end up having a scalable model for whatever you are selling. Part of your role is pure math. You either buy into the math or you don't. It's like shortcuts: shortchanging the math may work in the short term, but it will not work in the long term. The art of your job takes time to learn and refine. The art of your job is real, and that's where you get the repeat sales and the cascade of referrals. A robot can't do your job because it doesn't have the emotion or reflective ability to get better after each sale. You do.

This book was created with chapters that say as you do something, you will get better and you will sell more. That way, you don't have to use hope as a crutch to your success. It is you fishing—not someone else fishing for you.

Can you dream of winning the lottery? Sure. I still buy lottery tickets, though I don't expect to win. Some people may say I am wasting my money. They are right. I do get a little smile on my face as I hope I will win. That's the only "hope" I have.

Please abandon hope as a strategy to sell more, because it won't work. Each day that hope doesn't work, your anxiety and your worry build up. You may get a tad more negative and wonder why it is not working for you. Abandon hope and put in the sweat equity in whatever you are trying to sell. A great leader I know named Don says, "Get it done." Get it done does not rely on hope; it relies on the person in the mirror.

Success happens when you admit that hope is not a strategy and that you need to contemplate the creation of a multifaceted plan to have more face-to-face meetings.

## Vocabulary

Hope: the feeling that something desired can be had or will happen

Instinctive: (of behavior or actions) not thought about, planned, or learned

# Leader vs. Manager

The role of a manager is very important. I do not want to diminish the day-to-day work that a manager does or the functions that a manager provides. The ability to execute on tactical operations and processes is critical to the functioning of our economy. Daily oversight is needed to keep the machine well-oiled and working in the most efficient way possible. The ability to follow through on end-to-end check lists and identifying gaps is important to the company. Let's differentiate these two words (leader, manager) in a simple way. Great leaders are also very efficient managers, but not all managers are leaders. Maybe it is just me, but I bristle when someone calls someone else a manager when that person is really a leader. I personally see a huge gulf between the leader and manager.

Because of what could be called a personal bias, I wanted to spend a few minutes on some of the traits of leaders. I do this for a couple of reasons. First, as you think about leaders who have helped you, they will probably have some of these traits. Second, I'd like you to consider how you can adopt or evolve some of these traits so that you can become a stronger leader. Third, I want to highlight some leadership traits because leaders sell more.

- Leaders drive change to increase personal and corporate productivity.

    Group think drives a company to remain stagnant and in many cases helps the company regress. Leaders who drive change believe that change will help everyone. Change for the sake of change does not make sense, but change based on the strategic vision and tactical action steps of a leader inspires everyone. Leaders are not afraid of change.

- Leaders show *humility* in good times and bad.

    Bombastic leaders who thump their chests and let the world know how great they are usually are short-lived. They may have a good year or two, but eventually their act wears people out. Leaders who show humility realize not all the good things and bad things are a direct result of their actions. They are humble, and that leads to greater client and employee satisfaction—and selling more. Leaders realize that they are never as good as the final results if they are excellent, and that they are not as bad if the final results are poor.

- Leaders raise standards for themselves and their teams.

    When things are going well, that's when leaders raise the bar. They set higher aspirational sales goals for themselves and their team. They realize that the good times may one day leave, so now is the time to work harder, work more efficiently, and strive to sell more now. The best leaders commit to a goal that is agreed upon with corporate and then set an internal, aspirational goal for the team. They may not hit the aspirational goal, but they will most likely hit the corporate goal. Leaders are also intelligent to push back on corporate goals that are unattainable. A CFO may want a goal, but he or she may have no clue what it's like for the boots on the ground. The leader in this situation tries to protect her or his people.

- Leaders strive for openness; put another way, they seek to understand and to help everyone become better people and salespeople.

  Leaders want everyone to win. To make that happen, they need to understand why others are not performing at peak performance. As a salesperson, you depend on a chain of people to execute. You are as strong as your weakest player. Leaders who seek to understand their people up and down the chain earn more respect and can help struggling performers improve. If you are ever stymied by something or simply don't understand what you heard, pause for a few seconds, gather your thoughts, and say, "I really need to understand what you just said and why you said it. Please help me to understand what you just said."

- Leaders are open about what's working and what's not working, and they are willing to change to make everyone more productive.

  The "it's my way or the highway" attitude is unfortunately still around. Leaders who are willing to change and adapt based on feedback from clients, prospects, or team members end up selling more naturally because everyone is empowered by the ability to influence.

- Leaders listen.

  Boy, we all can do this better. Listening is an art that helps you sell more. When you listen, you learn, you understand objections, and you show your interest in your team members, your clients, or your prospects. I know that by listening I can seek to understand and not be inappropriately judgmental.

- Leaders prepare for uncertainty.

  Leaders try to avoid the avoidable mistakes. By doing so, when real trouble surfaces they can address the issue and create a process to avoid the same gap in the future. A guy named Don, whom I mentioned earlier, says, "Actuaries can tell you what percentage of people will die at what age level. Unfortunately, the actuary can't tell you who will die or when a specific person will die." Leaders can't prepare for every situation, but they can be aware that things can and will go wrong. By attempting to limit avoidable surprises, they are better prepared to act and thus sell more in the future.

- Leaders focus on the client.

    Whenever you are in a slump, you can do a diagnostic or a decomposition of the slump, and more times than not it is because you lost focus on your client. It may not seem that way, but the stresses to make margins, crank out that last sale, or tweak a product or service to save a few pennies eventually leads to an unhappy client.

- Leaders maximize relationships.

    We spend most of the book on this topic. Leaders that maximize relationships, not abuse or take advantage of them, sell a whole lot more than slick, quick-fix salespeople.

- Leaders think strategically.

    The barbell of strategy and tactics is real. Leaders leverage both ends of that barbell. What's interesting about leaders is that they will create and generate strategic solutions because they have the mental and emotional capacity to do so. They don't look at the job as nine-to-five and then turn it off. If they have an awesome idea at midnight, they turn on the light, write it down, and then reflect on it the next day. They give back without knowing the exact personal payoff, but they know it can only help in the long term.

- Leaders drive innovation.

  Why not try this? The film company that thought digital images were a fad made a mistake. Leaders are in a relentless pursuit to improve a product or service because they know that pursuit will lead to more sales. Look at how the smartphone has transformed our economy.

- Leaders drive business results.

  Leader never accept the status quo or mediocre performance. They want to sell more, and have everyone share in the benefits of increased results. Leaders understand that the entire team needs to produce to hit aspirational goals, so they try to leave no person behind.

- Leaders demonstrate accountability.

  Leaders accept the end work product—good, bad, or indifferent. They never cross their arms and blame the next person. They fall short on sales, look in the mirror, and course correct. As they accept accountability, they also create a game plan to not repeat the mistakes of the past.

- Leaders build talent.

  Leaders recognize that their success is not solely based on them. Once they realize that, they spend extra time interviewing more people, probing deeper, and making sure they have the right people in the right seats. They cut mistakes quickly. Leaders also do more than utter the words "personal development." I'm sure every year-end checklist has personal development or some similar phrase in the "next steps." Leaders actually execute on the personal-development plans of their team and build a bench for future success.

- Leaders manage performance.

  Leaders need to treat everyone fairly but not equally.

Take some time to let that sentence sink in, because it is an important sentence. If socialism worked, all you would have is average salespeople. You do not. Leaders coach up high-activity, low-effectiveness team members, celebrate and feed high-activity and high-effectiveness team members, and usually provide a quick exit for low-activity, low-effectiveness people. Leaders usually spend the vast majority of time on their first and second quintile salespeople—the ones who drive 80 percent of the sales. One day I woke up and realized I wanted to save the fifth quintilers more than they wanted to save themselves. It is a difficult lesson to learn, but every leader has to learn it. *Fair does not mean equal.*

- Leaders lead change.

    Leaders accept as fact that there will always be change. Once accepted, there is more flexibility for them to change, bend, and evolve to help the organization rise to new levels. People who ignore change do so to their own peril. Sometimes you don't get what you want. When that happens, you can gather up your marbles and go home, or you can accept the change and lead yourself personally. If you lead well through change, senior people will take notice, and that will help you eventually.

- Leaders build trust.

    Relationships and trust are a common theme to selling more in this book. If people trust you, you will sell more. If you abuse that trust, you will sell less, damage your local reputation, and damage the reputation of your firm. Building trust takes time, just like building a relationship. A fancy smile and a sharp suit doesn't sell more; having a trusting relationship does. I'm a believer that you give people your trust up front. You may say I have a bit of naiveté, but history has shown me that most leaders are good judges of character and don't get burned often. I have been burned. It happens and you need to accept it. The vast benefits you have earned by trusting people up front outweigh the times you get burned. Trust me!

- Leaders communicate effectively.

  Strong salespeople communicate effectively across all mediums. You may be better at face-to-face and would prefer to avoid the conference call, but you recognize this gap and spend more time preparing. Communication should be brief, to the point, and positive when appropriate. Communication should share the vision of why and the tactical execution steps of the how. It is better to over-communicate. Most great salespeople need to be told something twelve times before it sinks in. As you know, it's not important to the salesperson until it's important to the salesperson.

Most of the leaders mentioned in this book are the best of the best. I use a phrase for them: rock star leaders. Rock star leaders balance the use of head, heart, and intuition. The same applies for rock star salespeople. It is rare that you have the complete, polished package. We are all works in progress, and it can be suggested that anyone who thinks they are done polishing or learning has just failed.

Throughout the book I discuss how hard it can be to change, to get out of your comfort zone, to ask for help, and to provide help. I'm sure someone in your family has said, "If it was easy, everyone would do it." Just because you want to sell a lot doesn't mean you read a book, flip a switch, and ring the cash register. You need to change, and you need to work. It is hard.

What's easy?
- It is easy to quit and give up.
- It's easy to try something new and, when it doesn't work the first couple of times, go back to what you were doing before.
- It is easy to internally say, "I am 80 percent there, and that's good enough."

- It's easy to believe there is a shortcut to success.

I embrace and celebrate leaders. I embrace the fact that they sell a heck of a lot more than the average person. Now that, my friends, is special!

## Vocabulary

Leader: (person in control) a person who manages or controls other people, esp. because of his or her ability or position

Humility: the feeling or attitude that you have no special importance that makes you better than others; lack of pride

Adapt: to adjust to different conditions or uses, or to change to meet different situations

### Activity

1. Like a previous activity, circle the leadership traits you would like to work on. Consider a conversation with a leader who embodies a trait you want to emulate and ask for some help.
2. Star the traits that you are already awesome at. Ensure they are part of your elevator pitch.

## You Lose ... Don't Take It Personally or Overreact

Rejection is a big part of life. Those who have been rejected more than most tend to be more successful than most. They understand the risk-reward trade-off that rejection can bring, as well as the learning experiences gained from rejection.

Because we are all human, sometimes we take rejection personally. Rejection does hurt. It is easy to say, "Shrug it off, it is part of life," but it can be difficult to forget because we naturally internalize what we are feeling.

Besides taking time to contemplate why you were rejected, what can you do? You need to keep it simple.

## Pause

Despite a strong internal urge to act, to send that e-mail or text, to lob in the phone call, or to walk into an office, you should pause. Pausing before acting is a sign of courage and maturity. Please feel free to write down whatever you want and save it to the draft file—just don't send it. Look at it twenty-four hours later and then make a more mature, reflective decision. Every time I don't follow my own advice, I feel like an idiot. I have to call and apologize for overreacting. Skip the apology call and don't send the note.

## Count to Ten

If you are in a situation where you need to respond in the moment, take a deep breath and count to ten before you say anything. While a silence of ten seconds may seem like an eternity to your internal clock, that time to think may save your job, your client, or your next prospect. "Count to ten? How childish," you say. I'm asking you to trust me. Step back from your anger, confusion, and negative feelings and count to ten.

## Walk Away

Go outside for some fresh air and decompress. Walk around the block or sit in a park, but get away from the environment. When you are outside, don't think about the problem; breathe in the air and let your senses take in the external environment while taking time to compose yourself. I have diffused a lot of issues, many which I'd caused, by saying, "I need to walk around the block. See you in fifteen."

## Talk about It

Communicate with a friend about the rejection. Spend some time with an external coach to review the situation. Speak with your accountability partner and share your experience. What you can't do is bottle up what you feel and pretend it doesn't matter. It *does* matter, and that's why you are upset, angry, or confused and are saying, "Why did this happen?"

## Write It Down

Write down how you are feeling. You don't need a diary, but a recording of what you are feeling is helpful when you look back at the situation. It's like doing a Sudoku puzzle: you may get stuck, so you put the puzzle away instead of throwing it away. When you revisit the puzzle, you see an answer or a thread that will lead to an answer. If it wasn't written down, there is no way you will remember the exact situation later. Writing things down forces you to think.

## Don't Blame Others

Look in the mirror. Many times a sale is a team event. The reason salespeople tend to have the ability to earn large sums of money is due to the fact that they are on the front line, face-to-face with the client or prospect. You get the front-line results—win, lose, or defer. You bear the ultimate responsibility for a sale or the lack of one. Please don't fall into the trap of blaming others. It may make you feel better for a moment. It won't help you earn more sales or become a better salesperson.

## Seek to Understand

Do an autopsy on what happened when you lost. Many times we lose a sale, and we wipe it from our memory and move on. The most effective salespeople are resilient and have short memories. That is a positive, but it is a negative if you don't learn from lost sales. Many times we neglect the basics and try to go for the sale.

- Did I really listen to the needs of the prospect or client?
- Did I do a great job at overcoming objections, but I solved for the incorrect objection?
- Did I miss the timing of the sale because I didn't do a good job following up?
- Did I miss the sale because I was unaware of events occurring in the external market or competitive environment?
- Was I just too aggressive?
- Who got the sale, and why?

## Ask Why

"I'm really disappointed we did not make this work out. I've taken some time to contemplate what happened, and I was wondering if we could do a quick review. As I look in the mirror, I've thought about our meetings, and I would appreciate your viewpoint on the main reasons we didn't move forward. I'm seeking to understand so I can be more helpful to future clients and myself." As always, if you approach a lost sale in this manner—with sincerity and the desire to get better—most people will be honest and fact-based with you. When a sale is lost, most salespeople won't take this approach, so you will be viewed as unique. It may also lead to sales years down the road.

## Don't Strike Back

The easy thing to do when you lose a sale is to let the prospects know they are wrong, they made a mistake, and they will regret it. Don't do something really dumb like speak negatively of any client, company, or prospect. There is a reason you lost that sale. Being negative or acting like the glass is half empty solves nothing.

## Don't Go Away

Depending on what you are selling, there may be a propensity to purchase more, replace aged inventory, or expand into different areas. Rock star salespeople don't let a prospect get away. With technology we can keep in touch with people in a "set it and forget it" model. Send e-mails, LinkedIn touches, and video business cards. Once you have a personal e-mail, you can touch base every ninety days to say hello, let them know of a new product improvement or innovation, or provide a positive touch. It's free, simple, and thoughtful. It can lead to future sales if done in a professional manner.

## Memorialize

Learn why you lose, and you will start winning. One key that most organizations avoid is sharing all the reasons sales are lost. We naturally are optimistic, and to memorialize all the losses over the course of time can be viewed as negative. It is not. By gathering all the reasons people lose sales, you can uncover gaps you didn't know existed.

- You can uncover gaps in your sales process.
- You can uncover gaps in people who can be retrained or coached up.
- You can uncover gaps in the training process to help all new people.

- You can uncover gaps you were aware of but that corporate never took seriously.

When you quantify all the lost sales, the corporate people wake up one day and say, "Hey, we should fix this gap. We are losing sales." Consider being the early adopter to gathering, memorializing, and then sharing results within the company. It should not matter who gets the credit when you fix a problem—if it is a problem that you help get fixed, then you and your peers will sell more.

### Regroup and Gather Data.

- Is it a fundamental flaw in your approach?
- Is it the product?
- Is the completion superior?
- Is it your effort?
- Is it your belief in your product or service?
- Is it your belief in your company?

There is one key word to take away from this section: Learn. The more you learn, the more you will sell.

### Activity

The next time you lose a sale, page back to this section and work through this content with your accountability partner. If possible, also speak with the prospect to learn more.

# Public Adulation and Private Conversations

May I tell you a secret? One of the easiest ways to have people follow you, embrace your leadership style, and implement your game plan is to publicly praise teammates when they do awesome work. *Praising* people is free and makes everyone feel better. Why are people so afraid to praise people? Probably because the person who provides the praise may feel like she or he isn't getting enough credit. That is silly. When you praise people in public and when you praise people in mass publications or e-mails, you not only have the appreciation of the person being recognized, but you have the attention of everyone else. Your team will think, "Why can't I try a little harder to be recognized?" Then you see the productivity of the team go up.

It is rare that you have a leader who is willing to give the credit away. It should not be rare, but it is. You instinctively understand why it is rare. People are afraid they won't get credit by the boss's boss. People feel like they will be perceived as weak if they give away the credit. People want the spotlight on themselves because they believe if the light is on them, they are better. I just listed all the wrong reasons that someone doesn't give credit away. As you sell more with your team, give the credit away. Take the leap of faith and see how much benefit you receive as you praise other people.

### Praise Best Practices

- Praise people who helped you in public meetings and at sales conferences.
- Praise people in writing as you send summaries of best practices.
- Praise people as you create stack rankings of performance. Everyone loves to be at the top of the list, and a simple stack rank provides a lot of positive motivation.

- Praise people that may be in your company but in a different organization who helped you get stuff done.
- Praise people whom you normally don't praise when they help you, like the lawyers or the finance people.
- Praise people who normally don't get praised because their role is perceived (incorrectly most times) as minor.
- Praise people when they do something extraordinary with their work or personal interests.

Give praise a chance and see how much praise comes back to you!

The opposite of praise is providing constructive feedback. I have observed strong leaders provide meaningful feedback to help people grow, evolve, and transform. Providing constructive feedback has to be done carefully.

## Constructive Feedback Best Practices

- Constructive feedback should be provided behind closed doors and in a private setting. The feedback should be provided to help, not harm the individual. You want to help the individual get better.
- Please do not provide constructive feedback in large group settings.
- Don't hide behind an e-mail to provide constructive feedback. It is easy to hide behind a quick e-mail and move on. Don't be a coward—provide feedback face-to-face.
- *Never* provide *anonymous* constructive feedback. If you hide behind your words, your words have no meaning. Anonymous feedback should have no value for anyone.
- Don't provide constructive feedback for a third party as a way to hide. "I've been told by others that you have been arriving late the past month or so ..." You need to be fact-based in your feedback, and that feedback has to be real, not perceived.

- Don't provide half the feedback. Sometimes we don't want to hurt a person's feelings, and so we won't tell her or him everything. That not only just delays the next conversation, but it sets up a false sense of reality to the other person. He or she may feel he or she only has to work on one issue, and then everything will be back on track. It may not be back on track because you were not comprehensive in your feedback.
- Don't avoid constructive feedback. Conflict avoidance is the quickest way to average and below-average performance. If you don't provide feedback in the right way, how will people know they have an issue?
- Everyone has different sensitivity levels. Be aware that an "in your face" conversation may work with one person and not another. Sensitivity is a sign of strength, not weakness.
- Verify that the person with whom you are providing private constructive feedback has a clear understanding of what you said. You can ask people to replay back the main message of the conversation to ensure there are no misunderstandings.
- Circle back and don't assume the problem is fixed. If you truly want to help the person, use check-ins with that person— again, in private.

If you have been in sales, you know things will go wrong. If your team is involved and you need to have a conversation, don't overreact in public. Have a conversation behind closed doors with the core members of the team where the gap occurred. Provide the client or prospect feedback, seek to understand from the team, and then understand the position of the team or individual if it is counter to the client or prospect feedback.

Give praise in public, and give constructive conversations in private.

## Vocabulary

Praise: to express strong admiration for or approval of a person or something done

Skeptic: a person who doubts the truth or value of an idea or belief skeptical

Anonymous: (made or done by someone) with a name that is not known or not made public

## Activity

Is there someone on your team or someone who supports you in a different organization that you can recognize? Spend a little time thinking about this and create a list of people whom you can recognize in public, where appropriate. Thank them for their help and make their day!

# PART 4:

## The Diversified
## Sourcing Strategy

# The Math and The Art

The math and the art are two concepts. Both are important. No, let me correct myself. Both are critical.

## The Math

You have heard me mention the math several times. Now, let us go a little deeper. The math is the entrance to the party. It is the sweat equity you must invest to build a pipeline of prospects, clients, believers, product users, and centers of influence that allow you to sell more. You don't sell things because you want to sell them; you sell because you have a game plan to sell. One part of the game plan is a simple concept that I and people like me explain as the math. Like many things in this book you can substitute other words—like metrics, quantitative objectives, etc. Let's stick with math.

Really smart people think they can avoid the math because they are smart. They believe they can shortcut the math. Many times really smart people don't do well in sales. This is not a knock against smart people; each of us are smart in different ways. The knock is the inability to accept that a ton of sweat equity needs to be invested at the front end of any project. Many times you run into dead ends that are not productive. The dead ends include the countless breakfasts, lunches, and dinners perfecting your personal value proposition and elevator pitch with clients; the generation of new first meetings that turn out to be unqualified candidates; and the candidates who you thought were terrific prospects but can't work with for various reasons.

The math in this process simply states that you need to do this tonnage of activity to build your pipeline of prospects. When I led a brokerage office, I could tell the people who would fail immediately. They were the ones who passed the regulatory tests with ridiculously high grades. They could test well, but they thought they didn't need to do the math. It never worked out for them. It won't work out for you if you try to skip the math.

You must know the math for what you sell. As an example, in one business we want every leader to hire four people from the competition each year to drive inorganic growth. We know we needed, on average, eight written offers to get four people who would join the firm. We also know that we needed about twelve people to go through a rigorous, due-diligence process before we can make those eight offers. We know further that it is about a ten to one ratio of people in our pipeline to get twelve people through the due-diligence process. That math says we need 120 active candidates in our pipeline to hire four new people a year.

The math also tells us we need to see at least one new person a week. Too often people mistake a breakfast, lunch, or dinner with the same people as quality activity. It is not—it is wasting your travel and entertainment budget. To be more specific, the math told us that unless we had a face-to-face meeting with fifty-two new people every year, we had no chance of hiring our four new people. The math can obviously get tricky. Fifty-two does not equate to 120. Our math told us that we can't pretend or fake the numbers. It turns out high-activity, low-effectiveness people kept seeing the same people and didn't bring in new prospects. They had the appearance of doing the math, but they were really faking it.

As a leader reading this, if your company has no understanding of your company's math, then you need to solve that puzzle. It will be trial and error, but eventually you will get the math correct. Looking back years from now, you will be the father or the mother of the math. The early movers will embrace the math and will move up the stack ranks. They will like you because you gave them the fact-based data that they needed. The high-activity, low-effectiveness people will ask for help to become more effective. If this group buys into the math, they will be fine. The pretenders will loath your name, which is okay because you don't want to be associated with them anyway.

Some people will say the math doesn't apply to small markets or niches, or it is for someone else. That's elephant dung. I defy you to find a horrible market that can't be turned around by a rock star salesperson or leader. That person is parachuted into that market and starts to act on the math, and eighteen months later that poor territory is highly productive and profitable. Great leaders can turn around any territory in any market in this country. They start with the math, and then they work on the art.

Here are four key issues with the math.

1.  If you don't know the math, you can't sell more. I am constantly amazed when I see companies with no clue about the math. They are wandering in the dark, running into walls, and never understanding why they are not more successful. How can you win if you don't know what it takes to win? If the company you work for doesn't know the math, be an early and vocal advocate of learning what the math is. You probably won't be appreciated or have a lot of raving fans, because you will undoubtedly increase everyone's workloads. If you solve what the math is, do the math as an early adopter, and sell more, then you are the ultimate winner.

2.  The math doesn't lie. If you try to shortcut the math, you may have short-term success, but you will not have long-term success.

3.  Don't pretend to implement the math. Do the math, and you will sell more. Pretenders are eventually uncovered. If you really don't like doing the math, then you probably are not having much fun. There was a guy named Nick who told a

large group of leaders he just "succumbed to the math." He didn't fight it; he accepted that he needed to do the math and accepted it. Once you accept the fact that the math is real and start doing it, the job gets a little easier. Once the job gets a little easier, you start to have some fun, and you develop deeper relationships. When you develop deeper relationships, you start selling more.

4.  If you find that you are diligently doing the math but not getting results, it is time to raise your hand and ask for help. I have seen people do the math and not get the results. When this happens, you need to get help with your effectiveness, or many of the topics you would consider art.

As a side note, here is a fun exercise around your personal math. This came from a guy named Mitch. Mitch was speaking to one of my former teams, and he had them break down what they wanted to earn and then correlate that to their activities.

For this particular team, Mitch had them write down their earnings objective. Mitch then had them write down how much they made in the prior year. Following that, he had them pull fact-based data from that prior year on activity. For this team it was the number of phone calls they'd made. On a team of ten, there was wide dispersion based on many factors, including time on the job and effectiveness. To keep it simple, he had people who made $.51 cents per dial and others who made $1.82 per dial. Let's put aside the concept of effectiveness for a moment. Take the income goal and divide it by the earnings per dial, and then divide out by fifty weeks (allowing two weeks for vacation). You now have the number of dials you need to make on a daily basis to earn your target earnings. Every team member needed to increase their dial rates by at least 20 percent—and some by 100 percent—to earn what they wanted to earn.

Of course, increasing your effectiveness increases the value per dial. The exercise is valuable because you now understand your personal math. If you are in a healthy team environment, you learn a lot from the valuations other team members have. The Mitch exercise is valuable, and I encourage you to try it with realistic income and activity objectives.

The math is real. Ignore it at your own peril.

## The Art

The math is usually viewed as the hard part. It is not. The math is your buy-in to the game. It is unavoidable if you want to win and be a first quintile salesperson. You can't do the math three days per week; you have to do it six days per week. The sixth day may be catch-up work, data entry into your database, or thank-you notes.

The art includes your proficiency in:

- Becoming a master of relationship building and not selling.
- Being able to deliver relationship-developing questions with your clients and prospects in your sleep.
- Understanding the importance of "you" in the process and what you bring to the prospect. Your personal story, your value proposition, your elevator pitch.
- Creating and following a sales process that works for you with modification as the world changes.
- Embracing and learning from lessons in your life.

That's just some of the things we have covered so far. The next part of the book covers more of the art. Maybe this is a good time for you to pause and do a quick skim of the first set of chapters. If you are like me, you get excited about stuff and try to plow through it, and you miss things. Or you may be reading at night and are a little tired, so you skim through or pass over stuff you think is either boring or not relevant to you right now. Sometimes there is a kernel of wisdom you miss because you want to get to the end of a chapter.

Accept the math; embrace the art.

## Vocabulary

Mathematics: the science of numbers, forms, amounts, and their relationships

Art: the making or doing of something whose purpose is to bring pleasure to people through their enjoyment of what is beautiful and interesting; an art is also a skill or ability

### Activity

1. Figure out your math and write it down.
2. Track your activity or your math weekly; work toward increasing your sales.
3. Pick an art topic that you could improve on and work with your accountability partner.

# Case Study: Jeremy—Back to What Works

I have been blessed to work with many rock stars. They are not perfect, but they try very hard to not only win but help others along the way. Jeremy is one such person. We are not going to talk about what makes him a rock star, but we will talk about some of his learnings.

Jeremy is an awesome recruiter. Over a period of months, Jeremy was not having the results that he expected of himself or that were expected of him by his leader or his firm. He was personally bothered by his decline in success, and he internalized this. He first realized that he had stalled. If you don't realize something is wrong, you keep repeating your mistakes, and nothing ever gets better. This is a negative spiral from which most managers don't recover, but many leaders do. You need to be self-aware when things are not working as planned.

Many times things stop working due to events beyond your control.

- A competitor is a first mover on a new idea or concept, and you lose a segment of your prospects
- The government or regulators change rules that create unintended consequences and end up effecting your business
- An exogenous event occurs that was not anticipated, and you need to change your strategy

I bring up these concepts because sometimes things just go wrong, and it has nothing to do with you. When that happens, you need to adapt to the changes. That was not the case with Jeremy. Jeremy learned that he had become set in his operating rhythm, and over the months his effectiveness diminished. To his credit, he realized something was wrong and was smart enough to do something about this. Jeremy corrected his course.

A lesson each of us must learn at least once in our careers—or many times—is that we may be running on all cylinders but are not making the progress we personally expect. We may usually lead our peers, and then we slowly get stuck in the average bucket. Don't blame the lack of results on the external environment; look in the mirror.

Jeremy took his realization to the next level. He denied himself something he enjoyed until he was back on track. He became so focused on getting back on track because he knew his results were not a fair representation of his effort, intellect, or *desire*. Jeremy created some think time to understand why he stalled. One day out of the blue, he realized he'd stopped doing what made him a success. Let me repeat this. Jeremy realized he'd stopped doing what was working.

He didn't do it on purpose; he got distracted with other things, and he took on more "free" corporate activities. He put in the effort but maybe not at the same intensity as in the past. The reason he lost focus does not matter. What matters is that something important changed. He realized he'd veered away from his personal selling process and from some of the math. It doesn't matter from what he veered away; what matters is that he realized it.

This happens all the time. You get more responsibility added to your plate and have other priorities added to your list of to-dos. As responsibilities increase, people in your organization will expect you to deliver on different objectives that may take you away from your core job. You think you can change some things up so that the process will work better. Maybe you take your foot off the gas pedal longer than you remembered.

It really does not matter the reason; we must realize that something changed. When you stall, you need to take some private time and write down what you were doing when everything was clicking. You should go back to your sales process map and determine whether you have short-cut some steps. You should look at your math and see if you have been slowing down. You should look at the math of your peers that are doing well. Many times we do a good job writing things down, but we fail to revisit what we wrote. Once you start looking at each day, you need to discover what was modified. Then you need to do what Jeremy did: go back to what was working.

Jeremy recently was promoted to a new, larger territory with more responsibility. He realized he had to go back to basics with his team. He introduced and inspected a diversified sourcing strategy (the topic of the next chapter). He rolled up his sleeves and got the team moving in the same direction. My sense is that when Jeremy looks back in eighteen months, he will be selling more and having a meaningful impact on thousands of families' lives. He will have enormous personal satisfaction, and that will match his bank balance.

Please remember three things about Jeremy.

1.  He realized something was not working and did not ignore it
2.  He took the time to figure out what changed
3.  He proved it doesn't matter in what territory one works; a rock star can turn any territory into a success if he or she is disciplined, implements the math, and works on the art

Before we leave Jeremy, I also want to highlight some other areas that Jeremy excels in that you should consider adopting.

- He figures out how to have fun, even with something like an all-day, brutal cold-calling session. He keeps it interesting by playing for pencils or lottery tickets for new sets, e-mail addresses, and more.
- Jeremy fights for his people, but when they make a mistake, he will course correct. Blindly fighting for people who are not doing the right thing is a mistake.
- He is awesome at developing a relationship with open-ended probes.

- Jeremy takes personal pride in adhering to the math for himself, leading by example.

The glass is always half full for Jeremy. Many times he has a glass with half an ounce of liquid, and he has to find a way to add eleven and a half more ounces. Instead of thinking that he has no shot of winning, he takes up the challenge with his team and works to get the job done.

Many times we get caught up in overthinking a situation, and we take several steps backward. When you stall, have the self-awareness that there is an issue and that it has to be corrected. Many times what we have to change is minimal.

Have some fun, and change the situation!

## Vocabulary

Desire: a strong feeling of wanting something, or something you want

Team: a number of people who act together as a group, either in a sport or in order to achieve something

## Activity

You may not be in a rut today, and for that I am happy for you. If that is the case, I would encourage you to write down the critical activities that you are doing in a typical week; and save them to your computer and an external cloud resource. When you get in a rut, pull out your list and consider what is missing. If you happen to be in a rut, take some time to examine when you were not in a rut. What has changed or has been modified?

I would also ask you to examine the other areas at which Jeremy excels. How can you think about being more like Jeremy?

# Diversified Sourcing Strategy

If you are completely dependent on one segment of clients or prospects to help you sell more, you have meaningful personal and professional risk. Too often we get into an operating rhythm that may not be the most effective long-term strategy when we think about to whom we sell. Having different sources of prospects or expanding share of wallet with existing clients is a way to tamp down volatility, broaden out our network of raving fans who produce referrals, and provide a safety net when something stops working.

Please remember a core tenet of any successful sales organization: retention of your current client base is actually more important than expanding through your prospect base. Think about how long it takes to earn a new client. Once you have a new client, your job is to ensure that she or he is satisfied and is a raving fan. That will lead to referrals. Referrals are so much easier to convert than cold calls. This section focuses on earning new clients from diverse ways, but your first job is to keep the clients that you have.

## Your Personal Diversified Sourcing Strategy

I say "personal" because many times you can expand the areas you prospect or sell to in your local market. Your company may point you in the right direction but provide limited guidance to expand the scope. By creating a personal, written diversified sourcing strategy (DSS), you can leap ahead of your competition and your peers to sell more.

The main elements of your plan revolve around large segments that include where to source new clients, communication, follow-up, networking, referrals, and publicity. I will start detailing different activities in your sourcing plan. At the end of the section, I will ask you to begin writing out the framework for your personal plan. Thinking you can keep all this content organized in your head is a mistake. By having your plan written down, you can revisit it often and tweak where necessary. You can also ensure that each element of your DSS is not only documented but is calendarized so that you don't neglect or forget key elements. Jeremy from last chapter realized that he had stopped doing some of his DSS; he stopped doing what was working because he was so darn busy. That will happen to you. This is why it is imperative that you write down your DSS and store it in an easily accessible place.

Here is a secret. You can't pick one thing that you are awesome at (like speaking to large groups) and skip everything else. You may see short-term benefits, but in the long term you won't sell more. When you take shortcuts or avoid activities you don't like, long-term success will be limited.

No one knows what will work at any given time; that's why diversifying your sourcing evens out the rough patches in different market cycles. It is *human nature* to gravitate to activities that you like. In fact, we usually start with the things we like each morning or things that are perceived as easier.

Taking that approach can be a mistake. We had a team of dialers whose job was to source new candidates. They are awesome people, and I am proud to know them. Their job was to warm- and cold-call people. That is a difficult job. Sometimes the phone feels like it weighs a hundred pounds with hang-ups, voicemail messages, being cursed at—you name it. Sometimes in order to avoid how hard the job is, they would do follow-up work in the morning, return calls for information from colleagues in the field, and plan the next week out. They did everything except the core function: dialing. At the end of the day they found that they only made thirty dials in an eight-hour day. This was poor activity that would not get them paid. To alter behavior, the entire team made a commitment to make thirty dials before lunchtime. They got to the hard stuff first. At the end of the day they had sixty to seventy dials at a minimum, and the next morning they had call-backs to follow up on in the afternoon, which were easier than cold calls.

Safety Tip: Over the years I have learned that tackling the hard stuff in the morning is the most productive way to start your day. After the hard stuff is done, you get to do some fun stuff later, and this allows you to be more productive. The other positive is that you remove that hanging black cloud from your head right away. If you know you have to make sixty dials in a day but don't start right away, then for the entire day you have a nagging message in your head that says, "You still have to pick up the phone." Eliminate the black clouds at the start of the day, and then you will have more fun.

## Some Elements of a Diversified Sourcing Strategy

### Mailing with Phone Call Follow-up

Don't mistake mailing things to clients or prospects as activity. It clearly is activity, but it is ineffective activity that is costly, is time consuming, and has limited effectiveness. What is effective is the phone call following up the mailing. "Hannah, I'm following up on a letter I sent to you last week discussing our ability to streamline your due-diligence process and help your company increase sales. Does Wednesday morning or afternoon work for you for a brief face-to-face meeting?" Remember ABC: always be closing.

When you mail, make sure your list is quality. It is a waste of corporate resources, and, more importantly, a waste of your time, if you have a bad list. Ensure data integrity with your data vendors and make sure your lists are updated regularly. When you purchase lists, make sure you open bidding up for competition with several data vendors. I have found that some have better mailing addresses, some have better phone numbers, and some have more personal e-mail addresses.

Consider spending a little more on your list so that you can eliminate prospects who are not suitable for your product or service. Pick the correct lure, not the big net.

### Emailing with Phone Call Follow-up

How many e-mail lists have you opted out of? Aggressive or abusive emailers drive me nuts. E-mail is a tricky proposition, and you need to be careful with it. First, you need to ascertain whether it is appropriate to contact a work e-mail versus a personal e-mail. If it is inappropriate to e-mail someone at work, always ask for a personal e-mail address. "Amy, personal confidentiality is very important to me. I will have some information every once in a while that may help you, but I don't want to send it to your corporate e-mail. What is your personal e-mail address?"

The key to emailing is to have content that is targeted, relevant, and timely to your audience. "Nick, with the regulatory landscape, changing the disclosure of your compensation to your clients may cause some unease for you. In this e-mail I have provided some suggestions to help you through this process. Even if you don't do business with me, this will help you. I will call you next Tuesday afternoon to follow up."

Using approved third-party content adds credibility to your message and helps you to add value with content they may not have been aware of.

Leverage your drip (consistent) e-mail and mail strategy to highlight major success stories. Prospects will wonder why something happened, and they will become more receptive to your next phone call. When you have a large sale with a new company, ask permission to use that company's name in your drip e-mail. Your prospects will see it and think, "Maybe I should meet with Thomas on this."

Rock star salespeople have sent two distinct types of e-mails.

- Proactive. Have a series of content available that appeals to a broad audience; this content may be monthly or quarterly. This means you need to spend time thinking about topics that appeal to your target market and then planning ahead. "Chris, I was thinking about you and thought the content on recent travel regulation changes in Europe would be helpful to you as you plan your next family trip. I will follow up with a call next Tuesday."
- Reactive. A change in the environment in which you work is a terrific way to reach out to clients or prospects to educate and inform. They will appreciate the content and will remember when you follow up with a phone call. "While we always stand for what our company sells, recently you may have seen a competitor fall on difficult times. If we can be of assistance to you or your clients, I would be willing to invest the time next Monday with you."

## Calling

Calling people is a part of life if you want to sell more. You can't be afraid of the phone. Even if you are having no luck with a prospect, get the personal or corporate e-mail address; getting that piece of information is a small victory and you should be pleased with yourself. You can now implement a disciplined drip campaign that will yield you more clients in the future.

Here is what your introductory phone call should cover.

- Tell the person who you are
- State your goals and objectives
- Communicate a benefit/value to your client or prospect
- Explain your experience in the space
- Explain the type of people with whom you work
- Action steps: a face-to-face meeting with date and time set
- End with a thank-you

JOHN RICHARD PIERCE JR.

The key to calling is very simple: you need to do it. Do your calling in the morning and then move on to areas that are easier to do. That way you don't have the weight of "I still need to dial for an hour" hanging over you all day. Usually when you procrastinate, you never start your calling. Despite what you may want, calling is a key activity that needs to be done consistently.

### Warm Calling

Warm calling is a lot easier. "Amber, I'm calling because of a personal introduction to you from your friend Tracey. She thought I may be able to help you. I will be near your office next Thursday. Would the morning or afternoon be better for a brief introduction?"

Call back when you said you would call back; that shows your professionalism and attention to details. "David, I indicated I would call you back today at 2:00 PM. I have some additional information on those private colleges for your children."

Clients and prospects will respect this. They may say, "Liz, yes, I remember you said you would call today. Thank you. Unfortunately I have my hair on fire due to a crisis. Will you please call me tomorrow after four?" Those are the best calls because they will feel obligated to spend time with you when you call tomorrow after four.

What do you say when you get them on the line? You give your personal elevator pitch and then ask for a brief face-to-face meeting. You can only develop a lasting relationship with face-to-face contact. You can sell without meeting people, but the face-to-face is critical for long-term success and referrals.

### Past Rejected Offers

Things change, and you should not let rejection bother you. Some of the largest sales can be made when you follow up with people who said no to you. If you get rejected and toss the prospect name away, you are taking things personally. Don't take things personally, and don't overreact.

"George, I realize that we didn't do business together last quarter. I was calling to check on you and see what has happened since we last spoke. What has been happening in your world?" Open-ended questions will allow you to hear that the person they bought from last time hasn't called them since the check cleared, or the service and follow-up has been horrible, or the warranty didn't work out as promised.

### Dead Leads

Dead leads are gold. Many times people are not ready to purchase, or the time is not right for whatever reason. Things change all the time, and you need to be aware that something may trigger a person to buy from you. "Lori, I was checking in with you because we haven't spoken in six months. How have you been? Really? Wow, I'm glad I called. We should review what I have to offer because it seems it might make sense for you right now. I'm near your office in the morning next Tuesday. Is seven thirty or nine thirty better for you?"

The last thing you want to read in a trade publication was a large order placed by a dead or rejected lead. Remember that things change, and if you drip on people long enough with the appropriate material when an event occurs, you will not only be remembered, but your call will be welcomed.

### Seminars and Events

Many firms will sponsor client events. These are perfect times to have prospects attend as well. There may be an opportunity for you to speak and then turn it over to an external, third-party expert on a topic. When that happens, you look to have positional authority and gain credibility with your prospects. Your clients also can internally validate why they work with you.

## Centers of Influence

Later in the book I will dive deep into centers of influence. COIs are wonderful because they are third parties who can validate how awesome you are. When you don't have to say things like, "Take my word, I will take care of you," you will certainly sell more. COIs take longer to develop, but once you have a network built, you will sell exponentially more.

## Local and National Advertising

Depending on your budget, local advertising should be focused on your personal value proposition, not your company's national message. Local advertising has become cheaper via social media as well as Internet advertising via your web presence.

Your firm's national advertising hopefully strengthens your local brand and allows your prospects to remember, "Yes, I did see your ad recently."

## Trade Group Participation

Like COIs, participation in local, regional, or national trade groups allows you to build your personal presence, network, and get to know the most influential people in the industry. Participation may take time and resources, but being part of the group is important to your local and national reputation.

## Continuing Education Networking

Most industries mandate some form of continuing education (CE) to maintain standing in the industry. Look at these events or classes as wonderful networking opportunities, not the dreary prospect of sitting through another lecture or computer session.

A theme you have read throughout this book is that the industry is small. It doesn't matter what field you are in; the opportunity to meet new people in industry circles will help you sell more in the long run.

## Industry Recognition Event Participation

Make sure you participate in national, regional, or local industry recognition events. You don't need to be a sponsor, but you do need to participate so that you are seen and can gather important, competitive intelligence. At these or any events, volunteer to be on any panel discussion. By doing this you will get your name in the agenda and registration packet that everyone reads, and there is usually minimal preparation needed.

With trade groups, industry CE, and other DSS types you are being recognized, which is important. The more you are seen at industry events, the more credibility you build for your personal brand.

## Referrals

Referrals are part of a DSS, and they will be covered in their own chapter in greater detail. Safety Tip: Referrals are not something you ask for and expect results from. There is a significant amount of art involved with referrals, and you must be very careful about how you approach the topic.

The beauty of referrals, if done correctly, is that the client or prospect provides a referral to people who are like them or are worth more, or who can buy more than they can. When they are cultivated the right way, referrals never result in people who are worth less than the current client or prospect. I say "prospect" because many times you may not be able to do business with a person right now, but you can turn it into a referable experience for three or four new people you didn't know were in the market for your product or service. Referrals are earned and should not be expected.

## Position/White Papers

Internally or externally generated content that helps your clients or prospects can validate the value you can provide. Too often companies don't invest the time or resources to generate *position papers*. It is a very short-sighted choice to avoid this segment for several reasons.

- White papers tend to generate publicity that will highlight you and your firm and differentiate you from your competition.
- White papers can be sent for publication where you are the author, or a byline that the content was provided by you, allowing you to be read as an expert. Being represented in print is very important and builds your personal brand. You will find that the more you print, the more industry journals and publications ask for your opinion, allowing you to be in print again.
- Position papers can be used as a part of your drip e-mail or mail campaign, and they allow you to keep pace with your competition if they leverage this key tool.

## Locally Generated Publicity

Did you do something great to help the community, or has your company added a new product or service that may be appealing? Send an e-mail to your local newspaper with content approved by your firm.

News outlets are starved for content, and writing up something for them makes their job easier and may get you published, which can help you sell more. Although it may feel self-serving, that is okay. If you did something that is worth being in print, you should cultivate those benefits. Prospects may meet with you, and clients may provide referrals if positioned appropriately.

*Competitive Intelligence*

Leveraging competitive intelligence both strategically and tactically is a way for you to earn new clients. Every day you learn information, and your network can provide prospecting advantages to you when they tell you about changes in your industry or major news. Competitive intelligence is critical for your success and is discussed in-depth shortly.

*Social Media*

You must be extremely careful with social media. Keeping your presence professional is very important. You will find that your LinkedIn presence will generate new clients and prospects for you. For example, many times prospects will view your profile before they speak with you. You get an update on profile views, which will allow you to invite a connection or mention in a phone conversation that you saw that they looked at your profile.

Safety Tip: You cannot spend your waking hours with social media; it can be a real time drain. Focus on how social media can help you.

- Introductions to people you would like to know and are connected to your network
- Notes of congratulations on work anniversaries, birthdays, etc.
- Following company news of firms that you would like to work with; this information allows you to reach out and comment on the news

A key with LinkedIn is to make sure your content is fresh, updated, and relevant. Like the website that had nine-month-old content, you actually hurt yourself more than you help yourself with old, outdated content. Did you realize that over 70 percent of your prospects will look at your web presence and online profile before they decide to meet with you? What does that tell you if you don't have a quality web presence? You may be losing meaningful sales.

By now you can see the importance of having a DSS. Rock star salespeople don't tumble upon success. Most will have a DSS that is written and executed upon in a consistent manner. We end here where we started. The DSS concept is easy to understand, but it takes a lot of work to execute.

The best do it, and the rest wonder why the best sell so much.

## Activity

Take a piece of paper and fold it in half vertically. I would like you to write down what topics covered in this chapter that you are doing today on the left side of a piece of paper; these are DSS topics that you do in a consistent and disciplined manner. On the right side, write down areas that you are not doing. Then on the right side, write down the areas you are not doing on a consistent or disciplined manner.

Now may be the right time to meet with your accountability partner and develop a DSS if you have a poor feeling about your approach to sales. Share the work with your partner. Copy that paper twelve times and date the first page the date it was written. In thirty days see if you can add something to the left side of the page. Unfortunately, something may move to the right side of the page; it has happened to me. Please be honest and put it on the right side. Self-assess each month and make incremental progress. That progress will lead to a more disciplined sales cycle and lead to increased sales over time.

# Competitive Intelligence

In order to become a rock star salesperson, you need to know what you are selling. With that said, what you sell is only one part of the equation. Knowing your competition and what they sell is another part of the *equation*. Gathering competitive intelligence is part of your personalized diversified sourcing strategy.

Where do you gather CI?

## COIs

Begin to intelligently map out your centers of influence, which are covered in the next chapter. Over time, develop relationships with these influencers and groups; you will find that when you need an answer, they will help. You will also find that they will call you and say, "Did you hear …?" Your network will provide unanticipated CI to help you and your company.

## People You Have Hired

Any time you hire someone from the competition, do a data dump and learn everything that is appropriate about the other firm. Stay away from trade secrets, and obviously don't break noncompetes or nondisclosures. Learn and seek to understand everything about the former company. They now wear your team's jersey, and they will be willing to help and be seen as a team player.

## People in Your Role at Your Company

Harness the intellectual capital and institutional knowledge of others in your role at your current firm. Form a loosely knit study group where you share CI on a consistent basis. Keep your notes and distribute them to people in your role at your company. Different things may be happening on the East Coast that have not yet happened on the West Coast. Share and learn from each other. Please do not be insular and try to do it all on your own. I encourage you to spend time with your accountability partner looking at different sources of internal and external CI; this can help you to compare and contrast what is happening with the person who has your role in a different geographic region.

## Leaders at Competitors

Don't be afraid to have breakfast, lunch, dinner, or drinks with the competition. In every industry we face the same issues. Knowing who is going through what you are going through can provide comfort during tough times. Although some people may be skeptical, reach out to the competition and say, "I'd like to make your acquaintance. If nothing else, we put a name to a face and get to know each other. Let's grab a drink next week. Does Wednesday or Thursday work better for you?" One day you or your competition may be looking for a job. Your networking may end up paying dividends for your family, theirs, or both.

## Industry Publications

Sometimes we get bombarded with daily e-mails. Don't unsubscribe from them. Daily e-mails from industry trade publications provide more CI than most other areas. Who switched firms, who was terminated, who just earned the big sale, and who has some issues? Subscribe to as many of these daily e-mails you can in your industry.

Do a quick scan each morning and then delete them. I also encourage you to consolidate all the CI gathered from these trade publications and share them with at least your study group or accountability partner. Ideally your company will have a shared drive that anyone can access. If not, PDF the content so that it can't be altered and post it on an internal company website.

## People You Interview

Every time you interview someone for a position at your company, be prepared with a multitude of open-ended questions. Candidates want to please you, and so they will divulge CI for their company as well as other competitors. If one of your peers is interviewing someone from the competition, even if it is not in your specific work area, see if you can join for ten minutes to get a pulse on the activity at their company in your specific specialty. You obviously should not inquire about confidential information, but it is fair game to understand what's happening at their company, what has been changing, what people like, and what don't they like at their current firm. Find out about gaps or innovations. Be relentless in gathering data. Think about your conversation this way: they want a job, and you want information.

## Breaking News

Get alerts from Yahoo, Seeking Alpha, or Google on companies in your industry. If something happens there, get the notice first. If it is appropriate, reach out to your hot prospects, share the news, and book a face-to-face meeting.

## Earnings

Read every quarterly earnings report from your company and your competitors. Find out what went well and what didn't. Always read earnings announcements back to front; the company always puts the good news up front and has the tough news at the back. Also, when your company has good news, send it to your warm and cold prospects as discussed in the drip conversation. The more they see positive press, the more likely they are to purchase from you.

## Sales Calls or Meetings

Don't blow off internal or external sales calls. Although they may take time, you will learn what is happening in the industry. Use the question-and-answer time to ask questions that will help you. What competitor trends do you see? What's your view on competitor Z shifting its workforce to this new product? Do you see any major shifts on the horizon—consolidation, expansion, warning signs?

## Conferences and Continuing Education Events

Many times industry conferences have all your competitors in the same room. That is an awesome place to pick up CI at the bar or between meetings. Don't be a wallflower—use every minute to be productive and gain knowledge.

## Headlines

Seek to understand why you see the same firms in the headlines. For good or bad, there always seems to be key players in any industry. You need to understand what they are doing because they tend to set the trends for the rest of the industry. George, as discussed in a later section, is constantly seeking to understand, and that thirst for why allowed him to be an industry leader. Understanding the why also allowed him to form better decisions and position things differently because he understood a subject deeper than most.

## Become a COI

Many times you need to prove that you can add value to others before they are willing to reciprocate with referrals and connections. You may have a specific expertise or talent that will benefit others. Consider sharing that talent or expertise with others. You then become the person who others look to for advice or guidance. As you help others the natural progression is that they will help you or know of people who can help. By becoming a resource to others you end up helping yourself!

Phil Buchanan, the subject of an earlier section in this book, has a saying of: "Be Seen, Be Heard, and Be Read." This is a very powerful phrase you should pay attention to.

- Be Seen—engage with your industry and specifically with CIO's. "There is Phil again, he is everywhere!"
- Be Heard—speak at trade groups, industry meetings, conferences, seminars, and any venue where you will position yourself as an expert.
- Be Read—publish white papers, local commentary and other blogs that are read in the industry. You will be viewed as an expert and have an opportunity to be quoted in news stories.

Once you have a map of strengths and gaps from all three angles (what you sell, knowing your competition, competitive intelligence) you have the ability to position your opportunity more effectively. When you have that knowledge you can use this to your advantage. Because we don't operate in a *vacuum* you need to write down any new CI and share within your organization. Become known as someone who has their pulse on the external environment.

## Vocabulary

Equation: mathematics a mathematical statement that two amounts, or two symbols or groups of symbols representing an amount, are equal

Vacuum: in physics, a space without any gas or other matter in it, or a space from which most of the air or gas has been removed

## Activity

What groups can you join or participate in that are COIs in your industry?

Become a COI for a particular area to help others.

Select one COI group that you can start participating in over the next thirty days. Invest a minimum of six months with this group before expecting results.

# Centers of Influence

In your search to grow sales and earn new clients, centers of influence can be extremely helpful. Centers of influence are typically external third parties who can guide, influence, or help you. Their help may not be direct or immediate, but they help in small and nuanced ways that will end up earning you clients. COIs are a valuable part of your personal diversified sourcing strategy.

In order to sell more, you need to have other people help you. As you develop relationships with COIs, they can provide recommendations or referrals; they can help make connections that help you learn. They may also lead to the next connection that will help you. Many times COIs have networking opportunities that can last for years if you stay engaged with them. As you read this, remember that COIs are one part of a diversified sourcing strategy. You could easily fill forty hours a week with COI activities, but then you neglect the rest of your strategy. Be precise when leveraging COIs.

COIs are people and organizations that you feel comfortable asking for help. As with many concepts in this book, understanding what an COI is simple, but understanding the concept and translating that into sales is a lot of work. Let's look at some COI examples.

## CE events

Most industries require continuing education. These events are typically in large groups, and many of your fellow competitor colleagues attend. Not only are the events important, but the conversations at breaks, before and after the meetings start, and during drinks in the evening provide incredible opportunities to learn more about the industry, a new company, or recent events while you establish a new relationship. Consider sponsoring CE events where you are able; you will become an expert and called upon in the future.

## Rotary and Similar Organizations

Social organizations that have a cause or purpose bring like-minded people together. You have the ability to connect over something you both agree on from the very beginning; that makes the first conversation easy to start. For nonprofits or other social organizations, you do need to believe in the cause. If you don't, you will be wasting your time and will not help the community. Please don't join ten different nonprofits. Your time is too valuable, and what you can add will be limited if you are spread too thin. This COI works when you add value to a group over time. With all COI organizations, eventually work your way up to a leadership position or on the board, if allowed by your firm. This will help you to become an expert and provide influence to help the group and your objectives.

## Charitable Organizations

There are so many great causes for which people give of their time, talent, and treasure. Here is where you meet people who are working for a common cause. Very strong bonds are developed, and they can lead to not only more business but making a meaningful impact in your local community.

## Wholesalers

Every industry has a group of external partners that services the entire industry. These people tend to be aware of all the latest local information: who left a firm, who joined a firm, what's happening at a competitor, and all the local gossip. We will spend some time shortly on how Gene turned his wholesaler network into a pile of gold.

## Lawyers and Accountants

Many times you may provide referrals to other professionals and receive little to nothing in return. If that is the case, you need to do a better job explaining how you help your clients and prospects so that they see the value in the referral. If you keep providing referrals and receiving none in return, seek to understand why. If you are still empty-handed, have a fact-based conversation and tell him or her that your referrals are done given the lack of reciprocity. Maybe he or she will pay a little more attention to you now.

## Financial Planners

Many financial planners are fee-for-service and have a deep network of clients. They also have a deep network of COI organizations that may appeal to you.

## Host "Lunch and Learns" with Industry Participants

Information exchanges with industry participants are an amazing way to develop long-lasting relationships. I mentioned poking your head up once in a while, and these informal meetings provide awesome information while building a network. As an example, Julia was a newly promoted leader and started a women's networking group that grew from four to over 100 in less than 120 days. She stages quarterly events that have speakers and topics that appeal to the segment. This group that she leads has dramatically increased her prospect list and is a source of referrals.

## Doctors, Nurse Practitioners, and Pharmaceutical Representatives

The health-care community has a deeply rooted network of participants, and although you don't want to violate patient confidentiality, these professionals tend to belong to very specific close-knit groups that may need your service.

## Teachers

Teachers have an enormous network of people they know, work with, or have taught. Too often we overlook the power of a teacher's network.

## People in local city government

There is passion in community government that allows you to get involved and learn about how a local community functions and interacts across events.

## Industry Experts

When you go to industry-sponsored events, you usually hear from experts in a particular field. Not only is this a terrific opportunity to gather competitive intelligence, but you pick up on *trends* that may help you to do your job more effectively or allow you to be a first mover with a new product, service, or idea.

This list is not exhaustive. Every industry has different sets of COIs. Keep writing down examples that pop into your mind and expand your personal list.

Safety Tip: Don't be a user. Don't be out for a short-term fix or name. You need to view COIs as a long-term relationship where they can help you, and in turn you can see how you can help them.

## Spouses and Significant Others as COIs

Don't assume one person has absolute decision-making authority. If something you are selling will impact others, it is important to get buy-in from the significant other, spouse, or team members.

As you speak with your client or prospect, you might say something like, "This decision has a large impact on your family. Now might be a great time to have dinner with your wife/husband/partner next Thursday night."

When you engage the partner/spouse, you may get a quicker yes. You are also doing the right thing by keeping the entire social unit informed of the potential transaction. Many times a purchase has an impact on the significant other. Not including that person in the decision-making process can be a mistake. You also earn points and respect if you at least make the offer to engage the spouse. Clients may decline, but they will appreciate you wanting to include their families in the process.

Identifying groups of COIs in your industry is the first step. The next step is how you interact and start to develop relationships. This is your COI engagement strategy.

## COI Engagement

As you develop a small group of COIs, you need to stay engaged. You need to determine not only how they can help you but, more importantly, how you can help them. As your network grows, you can connect people to people and become known as a problem solver or a facilitator to help others. "You should meet Tony—he has connections to angel investors. Maybe he can introduce you to some new people."

COIs are where you will leverage your elevator pitch the most as well as your personal value proposition. These two elements will be told over time as you build your relationship with your COI participants.

# Case Study: Gene—Mr. COI

Let's spend a little time with Gene and examine his strategic and tactical approach to developing a COI network. Gene's claim to fame was leveraging wholesalers to help him sell more. He took a multifaceted approach.

- Instead of having the wholesaler buy him lunch, he bought them lunch. The wholesalers were shocked because they were typically used for their marketing budgets, not the opposite.

- He took the time to explain who the company was and how it had evolved. Many times industry participants don't have the full story about your company, what has changed and what has evolved. Negative things from years ago may still be the perception or what they hear from a competitor. If it is a perception to one person, it is his or her reality. Taking the time to explain what has changed is a quality, level-setting exercise.

- Gene spent time discussing his office and why it was great for new people. The pride Gene had for his office could not be faked. When his network saw that pride, they began to think, "Maybe Frankie would be a good fit in Gene's office one day." When they saw Frankie or Frankie had an issue with his firm, the wholesaler could make a simple comment like, "Have you been to Gene's office yet? You might want to see what is happening over there. They seem to have a lot of positive energy."

- Gene spent time discussing his personal brand and the value he could bring through his personal value proposition. This is critical because you have now spent so much time perfecting your personal value proposition. This is where you plant the seeds for future success. This COI will remember what he or she learned and can pass along as things change in the industry, when there are events or the unexpected happens.

- Gene then learned about their business and how he could help the wholesaler; instead of being a taker, he became a giver. People who provide services to you are shocked when you take your time to learn about them and what success looks like for them. If you want the COI to understand what success looks like to you, you need to understand what it looks like to them.

- Gene also went to events where other wholesalers attended in the particular COI group. At first you may be at watering holes with some of your colleagues. Conversations are started, and you begin to make connections.

- During basketball tournament season, Gene hosted happy hours with the wholesalers that were first class:

  o Hand-signed, wedding-style invitations sent for the event
  o Personalized name badges (no last name for privacy even though everyone knew each other) upon arrival
  o A brief synopsis of his personal value proposition, elevator pitch, and commitment to help their business
  o Personalized, hand-written follow-up thank-you notes for those who attended

- o Personal e-mails added to drip campaigns
- o Invitations to join his LinkedIn page as well as links sent to his personal website

The end results were astonishing.

Gene received all the latest industry competitive intelligence as it happened, and sometimes minutes after it happened because the COI knew Gene would be interested. Gene had third-party validation that he and his office had a terrific environment when wholesalers spoke with people Gene wanted to hire. Gene also garnered referrals on a consistent basis by asking, and he also had unsolicited referrals as events occurred at the competition. Finally, Gene was the first person to learn about an unhappy person at another company.

Building a COI referral network takes time, but the rewards are valuable. To foster a long-term relationship, you need to exhibit a few traits we have discussed.

- Personal integrity and competence
- Ability to relate personally, not just professionally
- Showing the value of the relationship for both parties
- Showing interest in your COI
- Being genuine in your approach
- Providing incentives where appropriate, approved, and legal

Remember, COIs can help you sell more. After the investment of time, talent, and treasure, the results can be extraordinary!

## Activity

A good exercise right now is to contemplate COIs in your industry. Think about wholesalers who are connected with other people. What trade groups are around to sharpen your industry knowledge and competitive knowledge? Who writes white papers or position papers, or trains on industry topics? Do you have clients who know industry participants? Who leads local business or community groups? Create your list and begin to map out your personal game plan.

Next, add all new COI individuals to your LinkedIn profile via invitation. Take all the business cards you gather and invite them to connect.

Finally, see if you can mail merge your corporate contacts into your personal smartphone so that you never lose them, and once again begin the process to request that they join you on a social network.

# Quick Hits II

## Slow Down—This Is What Success Looks Like

What does success look like? In one sense, there is no incorrect answer. For some, success may be selling more in order to accumulate a larger pile of cash for a second home, put the kids through college, or retire in a way that allows one to travel around the world for a month each year. To others, success is spending time with a charity that they have passion for in order to make a humanitarian impact. To some success is staying on a flat sales trajectory but working four days a week to spend more time with the grandchildren or to teach at a community college.

Success is thus different for every individual. Too often we get caught in the moment and don't take the time to consider what success looks like for us today, in three years, and maybe even in ten years. The problem with looking at success in ten years is that so much can happen between now and then. Although it may seem counterintuitive, it is actually more important to think about ten years from now versus one year. Do you know why? If you can create a clear image of success ten years from now, you can formulate your game plan to get there. The problem we all face is not spending time thinking about what success looks like ten years out. This kind of a problem—or more accurately, an opportunity—is another component of your personal art.

A common gap for successful salespeople is that they spend too much time on the here and now and not enough time on the future. One day you pick up your head out of your proverbial cubicle, and six years have passed by. The question is simple: did you have success toward your three-year goal, and are you on track for your ten-year goal? If you don't make think time, then you keep popping your head up, and another five years have elapsed. Don't let another few years pass before you write down what success looks like for year three and year ten from today's date. Share your thoughts with your accountability partner to see if you have realistic or unrealistic goals for the future.

The objective of this book is to help you sell more in your current role, but it may turn out that after you start implementing the math and the art, you realize you can't hit your three-year or ten-year goal in your current situation. If that turns out to be the case, you need to consider how to get there. Maybe you can advance in your current firm; maybe you need to find a new firm; maybe you need to start your own firm. You have plenty of choices. The key is making those choices while you still have the flexibility to do so. Getting locked into something and then realizing you are too long in the tooth for a new firm is difficult to accept. If you get to the point of saying, "Wow, I need to change," hopefully it is a few years down the road after you have built up a large COI network.

Understanding the corporate environment is also very important. The *annuity* business went through a massive sales spurt during the financial services crises starting in 2008. Most annuities provide a guaranteed income stream, and many protect the principal as well. Although they can have high internal costs, the prospect of an income stream and principal protection was very appealing for people who lost half their 401K as the financial markets melted down. Say you are at an annuity company, and you are a top salesperson making wheelbarrows full of money. Life is good, right? Nope. For the top salespeople, they sold so much that the company had some difficult decisions to make. Because of the guarantees of annuities, which are capital intensive products that also require a significant amount of hedging (or in the simplest terms, offsetting the risk in order to pay the benefits of the annuity contract in the future), these companies had all these sales that actually jeopardized the viability of the company. One company sold twice as much product as their sales target. Want to know what happened to the top five salespeople at one company? They should have been celebrated, but they were not —they were fired for doing their job too well! Can you imagine how it feels to be a star salesperson having a record year, and then your payment is termination?

The annuity example is one that stresses the importance of understanding the corporate goals and the ripples of selling too much or too little. Yes, the ripples again. Let's move away from your company and back to you. It's time for you to write what success looks like to you in ten years and three years from now. After you write down what success looks like, you have two things to do.

### 1. Based on your current trajectory and how your job is going today, can you reasonably achieve your three-year and ten-year goals?

If the answer is yes, congratulations! However, a word of caution if your answer is yes: have you set your goals high enough? It might be appropriate to spend some think time ensuring that your goals were appropriate when you first set them. Over time your expectations may change, or your lifestyle needs may change. Based on these changes, you may need to modify your goals.

If the answer is that you are not on track to hit your goals, I encourage you to modify your behavior by implementing some of the ideas in this book. The person who looks inside and honestly realizes change must happen before the next large personal or professional leap is a wise person indeed.

### 2. Are your goals aligned with your current company?

If the answer is yes, that is awesome. If the answer is no, you need to thoughtfully decide what you can do to influence your current company to get better alignment. If better—not perfect, but better—alignment is not attainable, then it is probably time to start planting seeds elsewhere.

Everything just discussed can only be thought about if you slow down.

- Take time away from the daily grind
- Walk on a beach, take a bike ride, or go for a long run in the rain
- Sit in silence, or do whatever provides peace and a quiet mind for you

You have to turn off your smartphone and let your head clear before you can really think about and plan your future. Do that, and you will sell more today, but, more importantly, you will have created a fact-based road map for your future. You will be much happier and at peace with yourself.

## Vocabulary

Shareholder: someone who owns shares in a company

Corporation: an organization, esp. a business that has a legally separate existence from the people who run it

Annuity: an amount of money paid to someone every year, usually until that person's death, or the insurance agreement or investment that provides money that is paid this way

## Activity

Write down what success looks like for you in three years and ten years.

Force yourself to take time away from the job to think about your future.

## React ... 13-02/2243

In order to achieve success, you have to learn to adapt to change. FINRA (Financial Industry Regulatory Authority) proposed a rule, 13-02, that was waiting for SEC Securities and Exchange Commission approval (tagged Rule 2243). This rule would provide written disclosure of compensation received by financial advisors who change firms. Although it is uncommon and unheard of for lawyers, teachers, doctors, accountants, or any other profession to be forced to provide, in writing to clients, what compensation they received to change firms, that is the core intent of 13-02.

Every industry has an event that can create opportunity to develop relationships. Usually less effective salespeople don't respond to changes that may not look like an opportunity. When there are changes in your industry, you need to take time to think about those changes. What does the change mean for prospects? What can the change mean to sales? Is there a second ripple after a decision on which you can capitalize? If any of the answers are yes, it is worth the time and effort to pivot and create a written game plan to capitalize on the opportunity.

Using 13-02 as an example, you need to have a set of tactics that you implement to adapt to a change. For example, as you make calls to a prospect about a change, you may say, "Sandy, what have you heard about 13-02?" Depending on the answer, you can react differently.

- If they are unaware of the proposed rule, educate them.
- If they were aware but don't understand the ramifications to their business, educate them.
- If they were aware and didn't have a concern, seek to understand why they were not worried about it.

Next, send them a handwritten follow-up note telling them you will keep them informed. Rule 13-02 was an event that allowed you to educate a prospect. Events allow you to e-mail drip, snail mail, and follow up with phone calls as events unfold. You become the expert who woke them up to a rule change that had impact on their and their family's life. That has meaning and will allow you to build credibility as you develop the relationship.

When an event occurs, you should react to it immediately. Waiting simply means someone else will get to your prospect first. In this example, those who have been paying attention to industry comments and feedback were positioned to educate if the rule was ever approved.

A funny thing happened to 2243 and 13-02. The proposed rule was withdrawn, and the regulators went back to potentially rewrite the rule. The education of the prospects was not a waste of time; many leaders developed relationships with great salespeople because they tried to help them by educating them. They added value and that is a great way to build a relationship!

## Activity

Are there events occurring in your industry that allow you to grow and increase your sales? If not, be cognizant when an event occurs and then create tactical action steps to help you increase your sales.

## Have Some Fun

Having fun with your colleagues is important to sell more. Most successful salespeople have a will to win, a desire to be number one, and a passion for competition. Make no mistake, you don't have to be an extrovert to have the passion to win. In fact, many "external extroverts" are closet introverts away from the job.

If you have not taken the *Myers-Briggs* in a while, purchase the tool and use it. It can be very helpful as you interact with your colleagues. It can help you to understand who you are based on the assessment and provide different approaches as you work though a sales process with a client or prospect. It is fun to understand each other's personality types and how one interacts with the other. I am an ENTJ, but many times I am an I. Use the tool if you want to know what these letters mean!

In most industries if you have a sales initiative—let's stay away from the word "contest" because people seem to think contests are not appropriate—everyone wants to win. To dispel a myth right now, you don't win anything; you earn what you get. My wife corrected me one time when I told her I won a recognition trip. She said I didn't win anything. I earned that trip. You earn everything you get, and you should be proud when you are recognized. You didn't win it—you earned it.

Fun can be defined differently for different people. Typically when you have group activities, you build camaraderie, trust, enthusiasm, and excitement. Here are a few ways to supercharge activity and have some fun along the way.

## Calling Days to Drive Activity

I took part in several calling sessions to generate new first meetings (future paychecks) and personal e-mail addresses (to implement a drip e-mail strategy.) In one day we generated a typical month of first sets and personal e-mails. Each ninety-minute dial session ended with a report, some recognition, praise, and some trinkets. The initiative doesn't have to end with a trip to Bermuda or a television. In fact, it really is not about what you earn; it's the competition and the recognition.

## Stack Rankings so That No One Hides

Stack rankings have a way of getting strong results. In one job they had a black book next to the leader's office. Each morning a parade of salespeople would casually look at the list and see where they were on it. They would also look at who did the most business the day before. That caused some conversations about how and allowed for sharing best practices. For someone who was number seven on the list of fifty but just got passed by the number-eight person, there was renewed vigor and an effort to get the higher spot back. Although it is not all that fun for the people at the bottom, this book is for the people at the top part of all those lists.

## It Doesn't Have to Be Big

I'd submit that playing for a box of pencils signed by senior leaders will have as much value as other things you can earn. That box of pencils will sit proudly on a bookcase in someone's office or in line of sight so that colleagues will see it when they enter the office. Being proud of your accomplishments is fun and will drive increased productivity.

I was in an office of a leader, and I saw a certificate that cost about thirty cents in ink, but it was in a beautiful frame. Joe's certificate recognized results, and it was signed by the president of the firm. Joe had a ton of recognition plaques and statues; the one he was most proud of was the one he earned that cost the firm very little but that provided intrinsic recognition that lasted for years. Anyone who walked into Joe's office had to notice his certificate. Joe also saw that certificate every morning when he got to work; that provided the internal push to continue to drive hard and sell more. It also put a smile on Joe's face because he knew of so many other people who didn't earn the certificate. When you smile, you have fun and sell more.

## Define the Game

Get input on what is fun for others and plan an initiative.

- Keep the dollar value low; it's not about the prize, it's that you earned the prize
- Have a definite start and end date no longer than one calendar quarter. Longer initiatives lose intensity and have a negative

JOHN RICHARD PIERCE JR.

effect if people have no shot of winning three months into a
six-month campaign.

- Try to have multiple categories that earn points so that the
  same people don't always keep winning. Usually initiatives
  are dominated by your top salespeople just because they have
  bigger prospect pipes. Try to reward a diversity of activities so
  that everyone has a fair chance to be at the top of the stack rank.
- If it is a quarterly initiative, report out on results each Monday
  morning in writing, at sales meetings, and via e-mail.
- Have the leaders share how they made their progress—share
  best practices as a group.
- The leader should highlight and celebrate outstanding
  achievement on a weekly basis.
- There should always be three winners: gold, silver, and
  bronze. However, this isn't a child's game—you don't get a
  prize for showing up.

You should also have fun mapped out for your referral sources and
all your COI buckets. Having fun with this segment relaxes people,
shows them you are a regular person, and increases the propensity
for more referrals. When you have fun, you should also be disciplined
about that fun.

- Just because there may be an open bar doesn't mean you have
  to get sloppy. When that happens, you actually lose clients or
  prospects.
- Follow the etiquette and first-impression rules that you will
  read about in a few chapters.
- Leverage resources of external parties to help fund your fun
  according to your industry guidelines. The industry is small,
  and the cross connections can help your clients and prospects
  as well as third parties.
- Recognize your COIs who have become your advocates at
  industry events, in group meetings, and in writing. You don't

have to say, "Rob gave me six referrals," but you can thank Rob for the strong partnership. That makes Rob happy, and others in the room will want to know why; then you can tell your story.

- Track what works and what doesn't work. If you learn that a golf lesson from a pro appeals to a broader audience, or a wine tasting or a spa day, remember that and work a deal with the venue for discount pricing if you leverage their facility multiple times. If something is a complete bust, don't repeat it. Many times events where there is limited mingling or interaction turn out to be a bust. You want events where everyone talks about how great the event is, because that glow helps you.

- Bring the spouses or significant others of your prospects to the events. Don't make the mistake of assuming that spouses or significant others don't matter. The spouse or significant other can tend to be the behind the scenes decision maker so be inclusive.

- 4/5:1 Guideline
  o Your investment in fun should have a four/five-to-one return. If you spend one thousand dollars on an event, you want to generate four/five thousand dollars in new revenue.
  o When you have fun, you need to ensure that not just clients show up. Sure, you can deepen a relationship, and that can lead to more sales, but you must increase your pipeline of leads with new prospects. You will lose clients: they will eventually die or retire. You need to replace them with current prospects.
  o Track the results of each event in your CRM and make fact-based decisions on what events should stay or go, and what types of people need to be invited to your events.

You probably didn't think having fun was so much work, did you? Making sure you maximize the value of the fun helps you to enjoy your job more and sell more.

If work is a constant grind, you will leave, or you will have high turnover. You want to sell more and have some fun. Initiatives can help.

## Vocabulary

Myersbriggs.org: The purpose of the Myers-Briggs Type Indicator® (MBTI®) personality inventory is to make the theory of psychological types described by C. G. Jung understandable and useful in people's lives

## Activity

What can you do to create some fun for you and your colleagues?

# Reinventing the Wheel

There is a common *lament* of people who don't get results. "If only I had ... I would be more successful." The people who are always in the lower portion of the stack ranks sometimes have a fallback for their performance. Usually they believe that if someone else would have done something different, or if the company did things a different way, then they would have been more successful. The argument may give them comfort, but it doesn't change the fact that there are people ahead of them in the stack rank. It is comfortable and easy to push results to the side and not only play the blame game but create excuses to provide personal comfort.

Thinking that you will be more effective if you redo the firm's marketing materials or promotional pieces is a nonstarter. I bring up this topic because I see so many people focusing on collateral and not the person in the mirror. Less effective salespeople try to rewrite things thinking that will lead to success. They view gaps as the excuse

SELL MORE AND SLEEP AT NIGHT

for the lack of success instead of leveraging the positives of a firm, product, or, more importantly, themselves.

From the bottom of the stack rank, you can't tell the rock stars how to do something differently. Besides the fact that you have no credibility based on results, how can you explain away other people's success if they are using the same resources? I'm sorry to be so blunt, but this is a hard question to digest.

This is not just about content creation; it expands into all areas of the sales process. If you don't believe in a diversified sourcing strategy, or the process to follow up on your first meetings, or having accountability partners, then how do you explain persistently poor results versus your peers or colleagues?

When you try to reinvent the wheel, you are putting up self-imposed barriers to your success. Maybe the process isn't perfect, maybe you need more support, and maybe you could have better tools. There are a lot of maybes we each face every day. What you do with your maybes will determine your future success. If you keep falling back on the maybes, you are stuck in a cycle of underperformance.

Maybe you should accept the "maybe" that rock star salespeople accept. "Maybe I should try to do it the way the best people do it, and then I will become more successful!"

The concept goes back to the mirror. Dave, a friend, keeps preaching that one's results are the result of the person in the mirror.

My recommendation is that you work with what you have developed so far.

- Your personal value proposition
- Your elevator pitch
- Your open-ended probes

First movers grab on, implement, and skin their knees, but they eventually rise above the pack and earn rock star status. Use what works and is available in the mainstream. If you have a record of success, and you start to try something new in your meetings as a beta test and it works, share your experience. That experience may allow marketing, finance, systems, and technology to think about how they could do things differently. Before you do that, you need to assess.

- Is the person in the mirror working as hard as he or she can with what he or has?
- Have I reached out to people doing better than myself with the same material to determine what they are doing differently?
- When I find gaps, am I fixing them, or am I plowing ahead and hoping for a different outcome?

Take a long pause and remember it is not about the material—it's about the relationship you build over time with your clients and prospects.

## Vocabulary

Lament: to express sadness and regret about something

### Activity

1. Reflect on the four topics covered in Quick Hits II. Stack rank their importance to you today, and then write down one thing that you would like to change or will change in each category.
2. Keep the stack rank and commentary in your book, and pull it out sixty days from this date; please make a calendar note in your smartphone right now. After sixty days, assess how you are doing against what you said you would do in writing. I can't call you to see if you did what you said you were going to do. I can try to teach you how to fish, but you need to execute on your commitments.

# PART 5:

## Meeting with Your Client or Prospect

# It Is in the Best Interest Of ...

As we start this section, let's reflect on who benefits from a sale. There are three parties who can benefit from a sale: you, your company, and your client or prospect. There are also combinations of the three that can benefit from a sale. It is important to understand who benefits from a sale because how you answer the question and what combination of the three will determine your long-term success.

## 1. Me

If the answer was "me," you will not have sustainable earnings in any sales career. It is true that if you said "me," you may sell a lot, but your career may be short lived. You know the people we are talking about: they get meaningful results in short bursts. These people tend to do a good job positioning their career, but they only think about the person in the mirror. These people are *shortsighted* and end up missing out on a lot of awesome things in life.

There obviously needs to be some benefit in this for you, your family, or your significant others. I get that. Rock star salespeople realize that they can't be at the top of this list for this question.

## 2. My Company

If you said "my company," that neglects two key parties in the sale: you and your client or prospect. It is interesting to watch the phenomenon of publicly traded companies going private. They buy out the public shares and once again go back to how they started while no longer answering to public shareholders. Inevitably one of the reasons given is the need to refocus on the client and not be so focused on the ninety-day earnings reporting cycle.

Is it important to do what is in the best interest of your company? Absolutely. However, to do that blindly creates an atmosphere of group think and a *myopic* view that will end in a cycle of selling less, not more.

Many times companies know that they need to invest in new products or services, but they are earning so much and everyone is happy at the top of the food chain, so they keep pushing back and delaying decisions to invest. Worse, they invest a little and roll out half-hearted initiatives that actually cause the company to fall further behind the competition.

The company may like it that you are the yes person who always supports the boss, but you don't help the company to grow and evolve because you go with the crowd. You may wake up one day with the perfect product that no one buys.

As a salesperson, you have an obligation to push back when your company is going down the wrong path. If nothing else, you will have peace of mind when the thing blows up. The other side of the coin is that they will listen to you next time when you have an objection. You can't be the guy who always complains about everything, either. Use your capital wisely and leverage competitive intelligence and client views when pushing back on an idea, product, or service. That's what leaders do.

### 3. My Client or Prospect

If you said "my client or prospect," you earn the box of pencils.

You obviously can't take this to an extreme, where you sell everything at any price. When you use the lens of the client or prospect, you have the ability to make higher quality decisions that benefit you and your company. If you were a client, what would you think about what you are selling? What would add value to you personally if you were a client? Always think backward or take the perspective of the client first. By looking at a product or service as if you were the client, you can figure out how to go to market with a better offering that will sell more and benefit all parties.

Try to look through the eyes of your clients or prospects and get their *perspective*. If you really know it's not in the best interest of the client, then you should figure out how to help them.

### Here are some ideas to help

- You should gather fact-based feedback; maybe your company can change something or modify a way of doing business to generate more sales.
- Probing is also helpful because you pick up competitive intelligence from clients, prospects, or people in your network. Your client or prospect may be buying something slightly different from a competitor—find out what makes their mouse trap better than yours.
- Testing a premise with a client or prospect also works. "Matt, we are thinking about approaching the issue from a different angle. Here is how we are thinking about this. What do you believe?"
- Have an external party send out your client survey to avoid corporate bias.
- Have an external third party conduct client focus groups for new or current offerings.
- When you get client or employee survey results back, actually do something about the gaps and celebrate in public your strengths. Fix the gaps and build on your strengths.

Many people think the saying "It's the right thing to do" is corny and trite. It really isn't. If you really want to sell more, it has to be in your client's best interest.

## Vocabulary

Aspire to something: to have a strong hope to do or have something

Myopic: unable to see clearly things that are far away

Perspective: a particular way of viewing things that depends on one's experience and personality

### Activity

This might be a good time for you to think about times when you made a sale that was in one of these three categories: it benefitted me, it benefitted my company, it benefited my client or prospect.

Then think about sales that benefitted all three. What were the drivers that differentiated each sale? Write them down. You will learn from them.

# First Impressions

I could write an entire book on this subject, but instead I have decided to give you some key components on your first impression. You can choose to use these keys and make a better first impression, or you can ignore the advice. Please understand that just because you choose to take the advice, it doesn't mean implementing the advice is easy. Jamie is a friend of mine, and he sent me a note after a conference call on a specific topic and said only I could have pulled it off. On the call we discussed men's grooming and teeth whitening—tough topics to discuss on a phone call. Jamie's recognition made me feel good. I appreciated the recognition. I also appreciated the fact that Jamie knew that it was awkward to ask people to improve themselves in sensitive areas.

## Appearance

No other factor affects a first impression as much as your appearance. Here are the topics I would like you to consider for yourself and your team if you lead people.

### Teeth

Are your teeth white? Don't have distractions that cause you to lose sales that are avoidable. Go to the store, purchase whitening strips, and use them. You can also keep an eye open for teeth-whitening specials from local dentists. Then you can smile and be genuine, sincere, and proud.

You don't have to show twenty teeth in your smile. You may be comfortable with a closed-mouth smile or just part of your top or bottom teeth. There is no bad smile as long as you are comfortable and genuine. Smile when you meet people. Smile when you say good-bye. Smile on the phone—yes, smile on the phone. People can tell if the person on the other end is smiling.

## Clothing

Do your clothes fit? Invest in yourself. There are many places that sell quality clothes at a fair price. Make sure you are presentable. For men there are plenty of stores that have the "buy one, get three free" sales. This is the perfect time to purchase conservative clothes that both fit well and wear well. It doesn't seem like women's wear has caught up to the Joseph A. Banks of the world, but quality, affordable clothes can be found in many places, including Ann Taylor Loft and Macy's, especially during sales. If you have lost a lot of weight, go to a tailor. If you have gained weight, don't look like a stuffed sausage. Don't be offended when someone tells you your clothes don't work. Mike told me one day that I looked like I was from Ohio—right after I moved from Ohio to Philadelphia. He then took me down to the clothes store and gave me some ideas on how to dress. Many stores offer consultants to help you. It is very smart to ask the store if it has a consultant to help you put together a professional wardrobe.

## Accessories

When you have a meeting and are carrying a briefcase, purse, or computer bag, please make sure they are clean and of high quality. You do not need a thousand-dollar briefcase, but have one that is presentable and not scuffed.

Please ensure that any jewelry and other accessories (like a watch) is appropriate for the business setting. Any large or overt accessory distracts from your impression and conversation. If possible, do not show any tattoos or piercings.

## Grooming

Are you groomed? For men, no chest hair should stick out of your shirt. Don't have nose or ear hair. Do you have a neat, clean haircut? Are your fingernails clean?

A similar concept applies to women. If your nails are polished, keep them polished in a neutral color and don't allow them to chip. Keep up with your hair, including cuts and dye if necessary. The goal is to keep everything neat and to not provide something for the prospect to stare at.

## Language

Until you have a relationship with a person, be very careful about your language. Avoid slang, curse words, and any jargon that could be confusing. In addition, be aware of the pitch of your voice (do you sound nervous?) as well as the speed of your speaking. When you're nervous, you tend to rush things. When that happens, you lessen your professionalism.

Safety Tip: I have a personal policy to not comment on women's clothing as a male. Find a friend who is a woman who can deliver a message. There is too much risk for a man to critique a women, especially if it involves too much skin, too tight of clothes, or too revealing clothes. Carole was my go-to person when someone on our team was wearing something I was uncomfortable commenting on. Many times people just don't realize that what they are wearing is not appropriate.

## Body Language

Body language is a topic of which many people are unaware. As we have a conversation we usually don't pay attention to it. What I find interesting is that when you start to pay attention to your own body language, you tend to notice other people's as well. This provides a mental nudge that says, "Am I bent over like that guy?" That mental nudge helps to improve your body language and thus improves your first impression.

- Posture. Stand up straight and don't slump your shoulders. If you are tall, be proud of your height; no hunching or bending over.

- Handshake. Your handshake should be firm yet not a death grip. Look people in the eye as you shake their hands. It is such a simple first impression that can go terribly wrong. If you don't look people in the eye when you shake their hand, they may be thinking a few things. "Are you shy? What are you afraid of? Don't you like me? Do I make you uncomfortable?" If you are uncomfortable looking people in the eye when you are speaking with them or shaking their hands, practice, or start by looking at their chin or forehead. The dead-fish grip and the death grip are both inappropriate. The death grip does not convey strength but weakness. "Why in the heck do you have to crush my hand?" The dead-fish or limp handshake is again a sign of weakness and a lack of confidence.

- Body Position. Don't be too close, and don't be a close talker. We have all seen the sitcom where the close talker makes others feel uncomfortable. Keep an appropriate distance between you and the person with whom you are speaking. Don't fall into the other close-talker move: you move back, and he or she closes in. Before you know it, you are boxed into a corner. The only thing that registers is, "I am really uncomfortable with this person." Keep your body at a slight angle so that you are not seen as confrontational. Stand a little to the left or the right, not directly in front of a person.

- Chin. Tilt your chin slightly down, not up. You don't want to be perceived as looking down at someone or one of the elites who always appear a bit *smug*.

- Hands. Your hands should be at your side, relaxed, and confident. Men, don't do the hands folded across your zipper. If you are uncomfortable having your hands at your side, do a Google search for "the Angela Merkel hand pose." Ms. Merkel has a habit of resting her hands in front of her waist with her fingers and thumbs forming the shape of a diamond. It is a studied gesture aimed at diminishing the somewhat awkward public appearance of this business-like budget hawk.

- No Change in Your Pockets. Empty your pockets—no jingling allowed!

- Stand Still. Nervous movement, wobbling your foot back and forth, flailing your arms, tapping your feet —these are all nervous ticks that you may not even be aware of, and they are inappropriate for first (or any) impressions.

Safety Tip: Have your accountability partner videotape you making a presentation. You will be amazed at what you see and hear. First, don't be embarrassed. You will see good stuff as well as things you really need to work on. That is to be expected. Even the most polished communicators can improve. If you are at the point where you feel, "I don't need to do that," videotape yourself. You really need to do this to make sure your confidence is not *hubris*.

## Interrupting People

Don't interrupt. You can be so darn focused on making a great first impression or comment that you charge in with your thoughts or comments. You lose all credibility if you interrupt people as they are speaking. Be patient, bite your tongue, and actually listen to what the others are saying.

## Table Manners

Before I moved to Philadelphia from Cincinnati, my wife, Shawn, and I invested in an etiquette training with Ann Marie Sabbath, author of *Business Etiquette in Brief.* It was an awesome experience that helped us avoid poor dining habits and embarrassment as we both started new jobs. I encourage you to invest in yourself with a similar service.

Table manners do play an important part in making a favorable impression, especially a first impression. Invest the time to learn how to eat properly, and please don't assume you know it all. Read and absorb what experts have to say. One goal of etiquette rules is to make you feel comfortable, not uncomfortable.

Safety Tip: Just because there is free wine, beer, or drinks at any event, it doesn't mean you should get plastered. Many careers have ended or stalled because of the open bar.

This list is not exhaustive, but it does provide a solid foundation to make a better first impression. Remember, all this stuff matters!

## Vocabulary

Smug: very pleased and satisfied with yourself, and having no doubt about the value of what you know or have done

## Activity

I would encourage you to reflect on your relationships that started out really well. What was the location and reason for your first meeting? Then think about how you acted and something you did or didn't do went really well. I would also ask you to consider topics in this chapter and reflect on each topic and how you come across to people. As an example, if you do not look people in the eye when you shake their hand, why is that?

I would also respectfully ask you to be honest and write down the areas on which you know you need to work. I know you don't need a computer screen of sticky notes, but I do want you to write down anything discussed in this section of importance and actually change something.

# First Meetings

It may have taken weeks or months of prospecting, and you've just completed a first meeting with a person who you would like to work with in some capacity. This may be the CEO of a company positioning a new concept that could lead to a larger job for you, or it could be a prospect that kept saying no until you covered all the objections, and the person finally sat down with you for the first time. You feel good about the meeting. You are pleased with yourself and how the meeting went.

At the end of the meeting, you go back to your car, your office, or your home and put all your thoughts into a database so that you don't lose or forget key elements of the meeting. You should send a hand-written thank-you note that you personally address and stamp. The best thank-you notes are blank inside, and you write a genuine comment. Then what?

In every industry there are salespeople who are high activity and lower effectiveness. They do an awesome job on the front-end activity, and then it stalls. They look like they have a huge prospect list, but what they really have are first meetings that never go to second meetings.

You need to embrace the concept of *engagement*. Engagement is the acknowledgment of your need to stay on top of an event or meetings. You need to have a deliberate process and focus on follow-up to insure a second meeting and eventually a positive outcome.

The average person will look at activity metrics and say, "Wow, I was busy this week," but he or she will not dig deep into the data. If you see the same people over and over again without selling them something, you will fail. What is the quality of your activity, and what is your effectiveness? You need to personally own the quality of your activity and the effectiveness of your activity.

A gap that average people have is the thought that a lot of first meetings are the key to success. I completely agree that you need first meetings. The big question is, what have you done since you've had the last first meeting? Too often we are focused on the next first meeting and forget that we need to have a process to engage the prospect to get to yes. Another way to think about this is activity for activity's sake. We are so focused on tracking, reporting, and logging the activity that we don't stay with the candidates through the process. As we saw with Frank, it may take ninety days or five years to land a client. What are you doing between those ninety days to five years? Stop the nonsense of discussing your activity—*do* something with activity that has occurred.

Here are the four most common gaps I see after first meetings.

### 1. There was no actionable next steps following the first meeting.

When your prospect has questions, don't give all the answers completely. You need to work to get the second meeting. Remember how long it took to get the first meeting? Why would you leave the first meeting without a game plan for the next meeting? "Based on your questions, I believe we should set up a tech demonstration so that you can kick the tires yourself. I want you to see how the system works and how the process gets executed. After that, we can have you sit with the actual team to see how they execute for our existing clients. To earn your business, we want to provide compete *transparency* for you and your firm."

### 2. No second meeting was scheduled with a clear agenda or purpose.

Remember that your prospect's time is valuable. You need to respect the value of their time and evidence that. Even if you don't use it with the prospects, you should have a written meeting agenda that you can reference; this shows you took the time to prepare and invest in their time. As you near the end of the meeting, you can easily transition into some agenda points that will benefit the prospects. By doing so, they will again see that you listen and paid attention to what they had to say.

"Based on what I have heard today, I have some follow-up work to do before our next face-to-face meeting. I need to deliver these three things. As I review these three things with you, have I listened correctly to what you have said and what else would you like me to follow up on? Okay, I'm glad that I had most of that correct. I need to prepare a written agenda for myself for our next meeting. Based on what you have said, it will take me about two weeks to make sure I can fully answer your questions. Does Thursday morning or afternoon work better for you for our follow-up in two weeks?"

Remember ABC—always be closing in a nice, soft manner to get to the second meeting. Even if you have to wait, face-to-face meetings are critical; try not to do the initial meetings over the phone. You need to see a prospect's body language. You need to make the effort to see him or her and not allow an outside distraction that is easy to accept, like another "important phone call." To put a finer point on this topic, think about the amount of time spent getting the first meeting. It certainly is easier to get the second meeting set then it is to find the next prospect and start the cycle again.

### 3. There was no structure or purpose to the first meeting.

It is so frustrating to get the first meeting and then leave with the certainty that you blew it and there won't be a second meeting—or if there is, it will be "Call me next year" or "Call me after tax season." Always have an agenda and a purpose for a meeting. It may not be to sell more at that meeting. If it is a longer sales process, the best salespeople don't even talk about what they are selling or the economics during the first few meetings. It's about establishing a relationship. You have to feel comfortable, literally saying, "Let's not talk business." Start with open probes. As you learn about the prospect, you collect information that can only help you in the future.

## 4. You spoke too much during the first meeting.

Your prospect has no interest in a second meeting. Please pay attention to the 70/30 rule so this is not a personal gap. Listen 70 percent of the time and speak 30 percent of the time. More on this topic shortly.

After you have your first meeting, it is time to do an autopsy on that meeting.

## What went well in the meeting?

Go into your CRM and put in all your notes on this meeting and on this specific client or prospect. The yellow pad does not work any longer. Get your database built so that you have a treasure trove of competitive intelligence and queues to help you sell more to each specific prospect.

Type in what made the prospect smile, what made the prospect laugh, and what topics (personal or business) where the prospect seemed really animated, focused, or passionate about. This information is essential for your next follow-up meeting or phone call because it is a soft way to start the conversation and continues to build the relationship. "Chris, I noticed you were so proud that your two kids have been selected to the state lacrosse travel team. Where have you traveled for tournaments?" The personal smiles or proud moments also allow you to purchase a lacrosse book written by the coach of Duke LAX to make an impact on her or his birthday or during the holidays. Details matter.

## What gaps were identified that gave your prospect pause?

In your CRM, notate where the prospect had frowns or pauses to questions. Did the prospect get animated in a negative way or when you touched on subjects that didn't seem appropriate? What topics did the client or prospect avoid or deflect? As you review your notes for future meetings, you can make sure to avoid negative topics while solving appropriate objections. Even if you believe you have a great relationship with a prospect, stay away from religious and political conversations; those two topics can be a landmine.

The good news about gaps is that they provide an opportunity to help show your value. You fill in gaps or turn gaps into opportunities for your prospect, and you show your value.

## What objections were given during the meeting?

You need to learn if the objections surfaced are real, perceived, or simply used to block the road.

- Real objections need to be overcome to get to yes.
- Perceived objections allow you to provide fact-based commentary that eliminates the objections.
- Road blocks signal a reason the prospect or client wants to slow down the process. Road blocks are great because you get to dig a little deeper on the reason for the hesitation.

Proceed to a brain dump in your database and write down any objection that came up in the meeting. Objections tend to be the to-do list for you and your team. Objections also allow you to position the next meeting so that you can solve the objection.

Please do not answer every objection a prospect has for you at the first meeting. Following up on objections will allow you to set the second meeting and begin to evidence that you are competent. "Zack, that is an awesome question. My team will get the correct answer and specifications to this issue. I don't want to guess and then come back and tell you I was incorrect. After I understand all the gaps you want me to cover, we can schedule our next meeting in a couple of weeks. I will be prepared to help you more specifically." Always make sure your prospects know that there is a larger, supremely competent team behind you to take care of clients and prospects.

Remember, it's not about you, it's about your client or prospect. Let's discuss your agenda. Your first-meeting agenda may be very simple and to the point.

- Thank prospects for their time.
- Express an interest in learning more about them using open-ended probes.
- Provide a brief background on yourself and your firm.
- Have a short success story of a client who is a fan of what you sell.
- Identify any gaps, objections, or red lights during the meeting.
- Repeat back to your client or prospect what you will do before the next meeting.
- Schedule the next meeting.

## Agenda Tips

- Your agenda should be written.
- You may choose to share the agenda with the prospect.
- You need a road map for the first meeting, and that road map is your agenda. The agenda is like your personal checklist and will keep you moving if the conversation stalls or becomes awkward.
- If you are nervous, get taken off track by the prospect, or lose your place, you can reflect back on your agenda and get back on track.

Please don't discount the importance of the written agenda to you and your prospect. After you hold numerous new meetings, you will get a feel for the topics and get into a productive operating rhythm. You can tweak your agenda as needed. After practice, you won't have to put in a lot of effort preparing an agenda because you now know the basic structure of the meetings. Like all good checklists, you may have the list memorized, but always bring your checklist. You need to review your checklist before each meeting to refresh yourself on the key topics to cover and what outcome you would like. You would ideally like a sale for every first meeting, but that typically does not happen, so you need to use your agenda as a way to build the foundation to eventually get the sale.

Let's ban talking about activity for activity's sake. Focus on new activity and then follow up on that activity. The key to success is what you do with that first meeting.

## Vocabulary

Engagement: an arrangement to do something or meet someone at a particular time and place

Transparency: the quality of being easy to see through

## Activity

Now is time to start writing out your first-meeting agenda for each and every meeting. If you have not been doing that, please start.

Instead of thinking about your past first meetings, I'd ask you to go back and examine every first meeting you have had in the past ninety days and see where they are in the sales process. Be honest with the prospect or client if you dropped him or her between the cracks; attempt to re-engage him or her, and then start paying attention to next steps after a first meeting!

# Overcoming Objections

Here is a guarantee: you are not going to sell to every person with whom you work. To make the eventual sale, you will probably have to overcome multiple objections during the sales process. Objections are an inevitable part of every sales process. Like the math, you simply need to accept the fact that you will have objections. You need to create a personal mental mind-set that relishes an objection because you are (or will be) prepared to handle any objection uttered.

Many times the most effective companies gather all the objections that have been surfaced and share them in a common database along with the answers to the objection. When you field objections, your personal mind-set is important as you hear each objection. How you respond to an objection, or how you are perceived by the prospect reacting to an objection, may dictate the sale. You don't sell a lot when you offend your customer.

Try to empathize and agree with your prospect's point of view. "Yes, you are correct. That is exactly how we handled that issue several years ago. Thankfully, we have evolved how we do things, and we have responded to our clients."

Respond appropriately and specifically, to the concern. You need to think about the objection from the client's perspective. You also need to answer the objection. Objections won't go away if you dance around the subject—the objection is simply reinforced and now viewed as a fact.

Safety Tip: Make sure you understand the objection. Too often you may be responding to what you thought prospects said and not what they actually said or meant. Repeat the objection. "Brian, I want to make sure I accurately answer what I believe your objection is. Are you concerned about the reliability of that specific product, or is there a different issue?"

Many first meetings don't turn into second meetings because you didn't do a credible job overcoming initial objections. Many times you did all the talking or didn't clearly understand the prospect's needs, and the prospect decided wasting another hour of their life on someone who doesn't listen is not a good use of their time.

Here is a best practice: if you don't know the answer, be honest and don't fake it. Don't make something up. "Angie, that is a very good question. I really don't know the answer. You just gave me my first piece of homework before we get back together for our next meeting." "Christy, that is a great question. I want to be completely fact-based when we get together over the next couple of weeks. I will have the exact data you requested." Remember, always soft close and always set up the expectation that the next meeting is inevitable.

The most effective salespeople enjoy objections. If they have honed their craft, they can anticipate objections from past experience, cancel out each objection, and move toward yes. Hopefully your firm has a list of commonly heard objections and appropriate responses. As I have stated, hope is not a strategy. Therefore if you don't have a download of objections, start compiling objections and responses. Then circulate them among colleagues and your accountability partner to add things you have not heard of or thought about. Keep this learned, competitive intelligence on a shared database.

Objections come in three shades.

1. Real, valid objections
2. Objections masking the actual problem
3. Road block objections to stall the process

You need to determine in what category the objection fits. If it is a real, valid objection, then it is your job to overcome the objection.

If the objection is not really what the client or prospect believes, then it is your job to clarify what the true objection is. "Margo, I believe you mentioned problems with the warranty. Is it the length of the warranty or the cost?" If it turns out the objections are road blocks, then you need to asses why. Is the timing of the client not right, or is there a different reason? Many times objections are perceptions from somewhere else that are just assumed to be true until you provide the facts. Again, asking the client to clarify is your best way to understand the type of objection and intent of the objection.

Many high-activity, low-effectiveness people think they know what the objection is, but they find out after the customer goes to a competitor what the real objection was. Always be fact-based with your clients or prospects; seek to understand their concerns and why they have those concerns.

It is important to not dismiss an objection out of hand. "Jack, yes, you are right, that was exactly how we did things two years ago. Let me take a moment to share the investment we made in these key areas to eliminate that gap." As you answer objections, always soft close. "Mitch, now that we have addressed that objection, let's get together for a cup of coffee. Does next Tuesday or Thursday work better for you?" As you address objections, it is a best practice to review each objection the prospect has. "Hannah, it was great to discuss your concerns and share my passion for this company. Are there any other concerns you have that could stall our progress since we have just discussed these three things?" That sentence is a closed probe. If the answer is no, you press forward. If the answer is yes, now is the time to write down the issue and address the gap at that time or at the next meeting.

## Common Objections

Here are a series of common objections that come up in every industry, as well as a potential approach for each. Some approaches work better than others, so my suggestions are not the only answer. Each objection you overcome should be in your own words and in a manner that is genuine and authentic to you. Many times it is trial and error to solve an objection. Let's try a few.

*I'm too busy.*

You do eat lunch?

*Everything's great.*

If you could change anything about your business, firm, or operation model, what would that be?

*Even if I were to move/buy, I would not consider what you have to offer.*

I'm sorry to hear that. In your words, what is it that we offer?

*I'm not interested.*

Any particular reason? Remember that the world we live in revolves around relationships. It never hurts to know people who can help you in your area.

*It would not be a good use of your time.*

Speaking for myself, this would not be a waste of my time. If I can help you now or years down the road, that is worth an hour of our time.

*I am happy:*

- I look for happy people—I don't want disgruntled professionals. You always want to know someone in your area to go to if there is an issue.
- What makes you happy?
- Really? I have never heard that before. How do you do it? (Be humorous and get them to laugh.)

*It's not the right time.*

- Use our meeting as another acquaintance in your back pocket, as someone successful in the industry who you can know if things do change.
- If things did change for you, wouldn't you rather make a calculated, precise decision rather than a rushed decision?
- What will change for you in the next six months?
- What is the downside of finding out more?

You may choose to show empathy to the objection and then share a personal story. Sharing personal stories makes you human and ties work and home together. The better your client or prospect knows you, the deeper the tie and relationship you have.

Selling more may just be coincidental to spending time with people you like.

Sometimes it is a best practice to not address an objection on the spot as a way to set up the next meeting. As you map out the agenda for the next meeting, you can position the objection. "Trisha, I owe you some marketing material as well as an answer to that gap. Let me prepare an agenda for our next meeting, and I will be prepared to answer your concerns. I'm in your area next Wednesday. What time works for you?"

Unless you had a sales epiphany, if your client or prospect has no questions or objections, she or he may already be at a negative answer. The converse is also true; some people just like to be difficult or ornery and keep tossing objections your way. They look at objections as a game. Don't get frustrated. Keep clarifying and learning.

## Green, Yellow, Red

Let's discuss the green/yellow/red technique. "It looks like we have addressed most of your concerns. I do owe you answers on that technical specification. Assuming we iron that out, is there anything that would hold us back from sharing an offer with you to proceed?"

- Green lights indicate the sales process is on track and moving to yes.
- Yellow lights indicate objections that need to be overcome or exceptions that need to be made to get the process moving to yes.
- Red lights are nonstarters. Your firm just won't change something. "Amy, unfortunately at this point in time, our firm will not change that policy. We need to press pause until something changes."

The tactic of "feel, felt, found" can be used very directly or subtly over the course of a conversation. "I certainly understand how you feel. That is how I felt before joining the firm six years ago. What has been great is that I found our firm is so focused on customer service that if we have any problems, we are committed to not only solving the problem but ensuring your complete satisfaction before we would move forward."

Always peel back the proverbial onion.

- Tell me more about that concern.
- How did you get to that view?
- I don't completely understand your question. Can you please explain a little more?
- That's interesting; where did you hear that?

Overcoming objections can be fun and rewarding. By being prepared and learning as you go, you will have the ability to diffuse objections and be on your way to selling more.

### Activity

Does your company have a list of commonly heard objections with answers? (This is an appropriate closed probe.) If the answer is no, it is time to form a study group of diverse people across the company and geographic territories. Then you need to map out the top twenty objections and create flexible answers for the group. Distribute the answers to the rest of your colleagues and gather more objections with the answers. That list needs to be revisited every ninety days with your study group.

Second, I would ask you to list the top three objections that you cannot answer. Work with your accountability partner or your study group and get more proficient on these topics.

# Case Study: Tom—The Listener

Tom is a very successful leader. As with most successful leaders, Tom is good at many different things, not just one part of his job. Many first-quintile salespeople tend to do every aspect of the job well compared to average salespeople; they can lead and manage. In Tom's industry he has to recruit well to bring in people to his organization. He has to keep the people that he has happy and growing. Tom also has to run a compliant business as well as hitting the corporate growth goals with existing clients. Regardless of your industry, you have to juggle many balls and the great salespeople can juggle multiple balls well. There was a time when Tom wasn't as successful as he thought he should be based on his past track record, his work ethic, and his desire. He could juggle four or five balls at a time but found he was dropping them too often.

Tom evidenced strong leadership skills, took a figurative step back, and paused. He took some time to reflect on why he wasn't as successful as he thought he should be. There are a few important lessons in this.

- Be self-aware that something is not working as well as it should be. It may be the nagging feeling you have, or an off feeling that makes you wonder why success is not following your effort.
- Don't ignore your awareness. It is so easy to push things to the side because you are so busy. You can mentally justify

ignoring the hard stuff because you have so many tactical things to do from day to day.

- Take time away for the daily crush of business and actually think about your situation; then act on your personal learnings.

Let's get back to Tom. Tom is great with people. He realized that after a first meeting with a prospect he wasn't getting second or third meetings. As you will see in the data-mining section, Tom leveraged his personal data and then compared it to his peers. He saw a fact-based gap, and his self-awareness was confirmed: something wasn't quite right.

Tom did an autopsy on his first meetings with prospects. He analyzed what he was saying, what his prospects were saying, and how the meetings were ending. Like a thunderbolt, Tom discovered his problem. It is a problem that many salespeople have. Even rock star salespeople have it from time to time. It is a problem I still have and have to work on daily.

Tom realized that he was so darn *passionate* that he was fire-hosing his prospects with information. Tom would get on a roll and provide some amazing content. Then he realized the prospects were not saying a word; they were taking in the fire hose of information and passion.

Tom was not *listening*.

Prospects became overwhelmed. Tom was saying all the right things, but he was saying them all at once and not where it made sense. He was telling the corporate story. He was telling his personal story. He was telling the prospect why it made sense to work with Tom and his team. He was doing all the talking. The lunch appointment or happy hour was over, and the meeting ended. He had not heard what was important to prospects or their families.

The light went on: he had to shut up.

It's a very simple concept. You have been in situations where you were on a complete roll, and at the end of the conversation you thought, "Man, was I brilliant or what?" You forgot the lesson of "It's in the best interest of …"

You also forgot the cardinal rule that the sweetest sound to prospects' ears is the sound of their own voices.

Tom began to positively self-talk in his head. Before every meeting started, he said, "Shut up, shut up, and shut up." Tom showed his passion by listening better and learning more. The prospects spoke more in the first meetings, and Tom gained important intelligence that he used to obtain second and third meetings.

When you learn to listen, you learn more than you ever imagined because your prospects start telling you what's important to them, their families, their businesses, or their futures. I know you want to tell the corporate story, your personal story, and how you can help, but this can wait if your prospects are doing all the speaking. If prospects are telling you their stories, soak it in, listen, and learn.

The concept of listening is simple. You need to force yourself to listen more—don't let your next response cloud what your client or prospect is saying in the moment.

Here is your new personal rule: Listen 70 percent of the time. Speak 30 percent of the time.

It is true that the sweetest sound to prospects' ears is their own voices. Start listening 70 percent of the time and see your productivity increase. You want your prospects to say, "Man, that was a great conversation." It was a great conversation because they heard their voice the majority of the time. Start shutting up and start selling more.

This topic is a tough one for me because I need to work on this every day at home and at work. I'm not going to give you any homework on this one except to ask you to think about the concept of listening more and speaking less. Have some fun and make a tick mark when you wanted to speak and forced yourself to listen. When you get ten tick marks, buy yourself something small as a reward.

## Vocabulary

Passionate: full of emotion

Listen: to give attention to something you can hear or to a person who is speaking

### Activity

Next week pay attention to how much you speak versus listen for one conversation per day, for five days. By paying attention, you will be aware when you are actively listening. You will also get better at listening if you pay attention to how much you are speaking!

# The Art of "Thank You"

While watching television one evening, I saw an interesting story about a café in France. The shop owner listed coffee on the black board, and the price was nine Euros. That is pretty darn expensive. Below that was coffee listed for five Euros as long as you said "good morning," "good afternoon," "good evening," or "thank you." The shop owner didn't report a spike in sales, but the customers were friendlier, and they sold a lot of five-Euro coffees!

The mechanics of the thank-you has been lost to e-mail, tweet, or text. The art, or the personalization and thought going into your comments, has also been lost. It is very easy to jot off a five-second response and then jump to the next item on the list: check the box, move on. When you do that, you lose the opportunity to make an impact or make another positive impression. It is sad because the value of a well-thought-out thank-you note has long-lasting benefits.

Like anything worthwhile, it takes time away from the next thing on your list, and it takes time to think about something that has meaning and impact. Time is your most precious asset, but it is also your most valuable asset. You need to be smart with your time. Too often we check off the box, which is an efficient use of our time. Think of a thank-you note as a way to personalize something to help make your next sale.

After a phone call you have been trying to have for a long time, or after a first meeting that took forever to set, make a memorable impression with your prospect or client. Don't wait for the next phone call or the next meeting. Do the unexpected. The *unexpected* will be remembered and appreciated.

Here are the basics of the thank-you note.

- The thank-you note has to be hand written. Take the time and effort to write the note yourself. Don't delegate to your assistant.

- The envelope should be stamped, not machine metered. Spend the money on some stamps and keep them in your desk. Pry open your wallet, spend a few bucks on postage, and don't try to expense it to your company. Savvy prospects will notice that it is a real stamp and not a bulk mail meter that shows your attention to detail—and to them.

- Your signature needs to be in an ink that is a different color from any printed material so that the prospect knows you made the effort. Printers today can make signatures look very, very real. I get fooled by bulk mail laser-printed signatures all the time. The giveaway is the perfect signature in the same color ink as the content. By using a different color ink, your client or prospect will know you made the effort.

- The address on the envelope should be hand written, not a label. Labels say, "I had my assistant do this; I just delegated it away." Want to have greater impact? Then you write out the address.

- I'm *ambivalent* as to the return address label. I personally prefer your home address label if you don't send a lot of these notes out, because it shows a more personal connection. The home address also shows them you are willing to open up a bit.

- I prefer note cards that are larger and in the wedding-style format. Nonstandard sizes get people's attention. When you get their attention, they will open the note and actually read it.

- Don't worry about your handwriting. My handwriting is horrible, and it takes a lot of effort for me to be neat. Please do not delegate the note writing to someone else. You lose the value of the effort through delegation.

- I'm not asking you to write a book, just a quick sentence or two inside the card. The message in the note has to be sincere and genuine. The note does not have to be long, but it must have impact. Take a moment to reflect on how you are feeling and what that meeting or important phone call meant to you. "Rebecca, I really appreciate the time you spent with me. I believe we can help you with your growth goal. Thank you for investing the time with me." "Lisa, I really enjoyed our first meeting and am excited to follow up with you. That is awesome news about your daughter and her college selection; you must be so proud!" Personalize the note where appropriate to show you paid attention.

- You have the option to send the note to their home or to their work. Sometimes a note to home may be viewed as intrusive. Other times sending a note to a work address is inappropriate because mail is opened or read before delivered. Use common sense as you decide what address to use. You will need the home address either way when you send holiday cards, birthday cards, and anniversary cards.

Once you embrace data mining, sending hand-written thank-you notes is easy, simple, efficient, and impactful. All of these suggestions will have a positive impact on your prospects and clients because most people don't make the effort to send genuine thank-you notes.

You may be shaking your head and saying, "Why did Pierce waste time on something so basic?" Let me tell you why. It is so basic, and yet nearly no one sends hand-written follow-up notes as prescribed. If everyone did it, there would be no point in discussing it. I know how many people don't do it based on how many meetings I have had with people wanting to sell me stuff.

Make the effort, and you'll have an impact.

## Vocabulary

Unexpected: not expected; surprising

Ambivalent: having two opposing feelings at the same time, or being uncertain about how you feel

### Activity

My request to you is simple. Purchase fifty cards and stamps and start following this very basic process. If you don't get comments about your cards, I will be shocked. Writing thank-you notes is a lost art that needs to be started again—by you, today.

# Referrals

The concept of a diversified sourcing strategy is an important element to create a pipeline of prospects that will eventually turn into clients. I discussed referrals within the DSS chapter. A *referral* is a beautiful gift because it makes your job so much easier to sell more. You can earn referrals from all of the segments in your DSS. I say "earn" because you need to create a referable experience that is both repeatable and positive for your clients or prospects.

I worked at a company that kept track of client satisfaction. What they learned was that clients who did a certain activity were 97 percent more likely to refer similar or higher net worth clients compared to clients who did not do that activity. The data confirmed that if you have a holistic relationship with clients or prospects, they will help you to grow through referrals. That is exactly what you want. You want satisfied clients who will help you grow by giving you a chance to work with people just like them!

## Steps to Earning Referrals

1.  Given what you do, are you providing the right level of service so that you are generating referrals? If the answer is no, you need to fix the client experience so that your clients and all COIs are proud of sending you referrals.
2.  Do you have a fear of rejection? Too often you asked for referrals and didn't get anything in return. It may be the way you asked, or because of how you run your business, or maybe

it was simply not the right time for the client or prospect. You got rejected and then you stopped asking. It's time to start asking again.

3. You have to ask the right way. I will discuss that in referral best practices shortly.

4. You need to set a goal for how many referrals you want to earn each month.

5. Then you have to track the goal. Did you earn your number of referrals for last month?

6. Evaluate where your referrals typically came from and learn from that. Maybe you earned some client referrals but nothing from a local chapter meeting or a wholesaler. How do you course correct to add that segment?

Written this way, referrals seem fairly easy because we all believe we should earn referrals based on how we work. Unfortunately, many of us are not getting enough referrals, so we may be skipping some of the basic steps outlined above.

## Referral Sources

Let's take a step back. Referrals are awesome because people who provide referrals provide you with people who are like themselves or wealthier/having greater purchasing power than themselves. Rarely do clients provide a referral of someone with less money or less purchasing power than they have. For clients, it like a defense mechanism: they don't want to provide you with a dead-end referral because it makes them look cheap or ineffective.

At the end of each meeting (preferably face-to-face), ask your clients to introduce you to individuals who are similar to them or fit into a specific target segment that you have identified in your DSS. It is important for you to identify people who they would know ahead of time. You will gather this information over time by listening and leveraging your open-probed questioning.

You should also ask your clients for advice. Explain how you want to increase sales and get their thoughts on how to do so. A referral conversation can flow smoothly from the advice conversation. As clients make the referral, ask permission to use their names in the phone call or the letter you send. Ideally, you would ask your clients to facilitate an introduction over a lunch, or invite them to a seminar or COI meeting you will be attending.

A best practice is to put a message at the bottom of your e-mail that says something like, "The greatest compliment is an introduction to a friend so that I can help them." The same holds true for your personal website and any other social media you are eligible to use in your industry. Always provide the hyperlink to your personal website so that prospects can see how you run your business and how it may benefit them.

For more traditional ways of getting referrals from clients, consider coordinating client events, such as wine tastings, spa days, master gardening workshops, or golf swing coaching. Be careful with sporting events; sometime they are a turn-off and neglect a segment that you want to attract. Ensure that all your information is located on your website for any client or prospect event. Once your clients and prospects get used to visiting your website, they will encourage their friends to visit as well.

Prospects tell most industry experts that 70 percent of them won't meet with you until they've reviewed your web presence and your personal website. That's why everything you do needs to be updated to put your best foot forward with potential clients.

Sometimes you are able to offer some value in exchange for a referral. Please be careful because many industries have tightened up what is or is not allowable. But as an example, here are a few things to consider.

- Reciprocal referrals
- Educational seminars for their company
- Complimentary services

- Deferral of service cost
- Resource sharing
- Expense sharing
- Fee arrangements within industry accepted guidelines

Every industry is different, so please be careful if you are exchanging anything for referrals. It is always a best practice to review what you are thinking with your internal legal or compliance team in order to make sure you are within the boundaries of what is allowable in your industry. Once approved (preferably in writing to protect you), keep the affirmation e-mail just in case.

## Referral Best Practices

- State that you are accepting referrals in every correspondence to a client or a prospect, as well as on your business card or electronic business card
- Leverage the white papers discussed earlier as a way to introduce yourself to prospects facilitated by your current clients
- Encourage prospects and clients to send your position papers and news updates to anyone they believe is appropriate
- Have a section on your website where it is easy for a client to submit a referral
- Have a list of products and services that you provide printed on a business-card format with your direct phone number, e-mail address, and website
- When you provide extraordinary service or facilitate an amazing event, don't let the moment pass over—position the value you provide for referrals to strengthen and build your business
- Leverage LinkedIn for prospects who could become clients and who have connections with existing clients; ensure your profile positions the acceptance of referrals

- o Be specific: "Fran, I noticed that you are linked with Annie. I would really like to meet Annie. Let's schedule a lunch to make that connection."
  - o A specific request of a person's name is a much more powerful referral generator compared to "Who do you know?"
- Leverage people you purchase resources from to tell your story (Gene's wholesaler example); they may sell to prospects who become your clients
- Consider the concept of giving referrals to get referrals
- Always thank your clients or prospects who provide referrals to you; recognize them verbally and with a hand-written thank-you note.
- Leverage the "Google machine" and see how other industries mine referrals

Referrals tend to be your most effective client-acquisition strategy that will help you sell more.

## Vocabulary

Referral: an act of sending someone or something to a person or place where what is wanted or needed can be obtained

## Activity

Start by writing down your new referral strategy. Who are the main segments that you are going to approach?

Then, quantify in writing how many referrals you want to earn in a month.

Finally, start to implement your new referral system. Commit six months to implementing this system on a consistent (preferable daily) basis. Trying something for thirty days will not work. Be patient and work on this strategy for the next six months.

# Presentation Best Practices

The offer is the time when you are making your presentation in an attempt to earn a sale or to influence an outcome. This is a critical time because it is the culmination of your work, from the initial call and initial meeting to the arrival point of yes.

**Presentation Best Practices**

- If your offer will be in a written form, consider having a professional binder or presentation packet that not only outlines the offer but also includes any additional benefits that the client will have by working with you or your team. It always saddens me when I hear that people lost a sale because they had a poor offer presentation, or they took the offer and slid it across the table instead of providing an awesome experience for the prospect or client.

- You should control the environment where the offer is made; typically lunch or dinner at a nice restaurant for meaningful transactions. Try to stay away from crowded or loud environments. Opt for a quieter, more secluded part of the venue. Wherever the venue is, arrive early and ensure an appropriate location ahead of the prospect's arrival.

- Present the offer face-to-face and include any team member who can help in the closing process. Face-to-face presentations are critical because you have the ability to not only hear a prospects response but observe body language. You also can extend the meeting when it is face-to-face versus a phone conversation that is easier to end.

- Consider inviting the prospect's spouse or significant other, if appropriate. Many times there is more than one decision maker to a sale, even if it is an informal influencer.

- Leverage a "consultative versus sales" approach. This tends to produce higher closing rates. When you are solving a problem and enabling a vision, you are acting as a consultant, not a salesperson.

- As you walk the prospect through the offer, be sure to highlight benefits that may also be provided with the offer. Each industry is different, but extended warranties, guarantees, service agreements, and service and support all need to be highlighted.

- During the offer process, make sure you let prospects know how much you have enjoyed getting to know them and how much you look forward to working with them not just today but for years to come.

- Articulate the offer and opportunity in the best interest of the prospect, their family, or their company.

- Set a time frame for the decision. It is important to have a time frame that can be flexible, versus an open-ended offer. If the offer has an expiration date, ensure that is covered in your presentation.

- Be prepared for objections or hesitations. As you make more offers, you will become adept at knowing what gaps typically occur. If you are new to a role, leverage tenured people in your role to have them help you anticipate objections.

- Schedule next steps on the spot. Don't leave the meeting without the next meeting scheduled.

- Always remember to ask for acceptance. They may not be prepared to answer in the affirmative on the spot, but not asking them to say yes is a rookie mistake.

Be prepared and be confident. You are almost to yes!

## Activity

1. Review your current offer presentation and consider leveraging some of these best practices.
2. Memorialize your offer presentation in writing and share with your accountability partner for feedback.

# PART 6:

## Evaluating Why Sales Are Not Increasing

# Case Study: Jamie—Be Prepared

Here is the main point of this section: Jamie is prepared. Like the thank-you note concept, the concept of this chapter is simple and to the point. The more prepared you are for the expected and unexpected, the greater the chance of a sale or advancing your relationship-development process.

Jamie assumes he will get to yes at the first meeting. In case that happens, he will have every piece of paper or electronic document needed to move forward. Too many people are not prepared for yes right away; Jamie is prepared. As part of his first-meeting agenda, he has a section on documentation. Although it may seem counterintuitive to building relationships, every once in a while you have a client or a prospect who is ready and willing to accept your idea or make a purchase. I have seen too many salespeople push out a sale because the client or prospect is not following the normal relationship-building process. Unfortunately, if you do not make the sale when the prospect is ready, you may lose the sale.

One of the teams I used to lead was responsible for setting appointments for professional recruiters. What we learned over six years was that our meeting rate dramatically changed when a recruiter missed an appointment. If the team made an appointment and had to change it, we only rescheduled that specific appointment 40 percent of the time. That meant six out of ten people were never seen. That same point-of-sales ratio applies when your candidate wants to make a purchase. If you don't make the sale, you have two key things that can go wrong: your clients change their minds, or too much time passes and a competitor gets the sale. Be prepared to make the sale at that point in time.

Jamie also doesn't let the prospect dictate the terms. By this I mean that if there is paperwork to be filled out, he never sends it in the mail or via e-mail. He never leaves paperwork with the prospect and says, "Send it back to me." Jamie has learned to do everything with the prospect on the spot. The minute you leave a meeting, that prospect's phone or computer is blowing up. The paperwork then sits on a desk and gathers dust until the next meeting.

Being prepared is not just about the paperwork. It is about what can go wrong in the meeting. By that I mean your ability to anticipate and overcome the objections that may come up. When I first introduced recruiting to a company the leaders didn't know what kind of objections they would encounter. They didn't know how they were viewed versus a competitor. They didn't know whether what they had to offer was competitive. Over time they became proficient at anticipating what a client or prospect would say. Because of this, they were prepared to answer once they truly understood a concern, objection, or question.

A simple solution for you is to be as prepared as Jamie is. Have what you need in your car. Have a set of what you need in your purse, briefcase, or folio. Have what you need on your tablet or thumb drive. Learn by doing, which will allow you to anticipate the next question, concern, or objection. By being just a little more prepared, maybe you make an extra sale each month.

As I wrote this section on Jamie, I also realized that he exhibits the traits that you need to exhibit in addition to being prepared. I truly believe you need to reread things to have them sink in. That is why I am going to augment this section with the traits that I think about when I discuss Jamie or many of the leaders in this book.

## Ten Traits of Rock Star Leaders

### 1. Willingness to be an early adopter

Many times early adopters learn difficult lessons as they adopt a new strategy. That is awesome for the organization because early adopters blaze the trail and help the organization to adjust, learn, and train other leaders. Being an early adopter is not easy because you tend to fail, learn, fail again, and then get results. As an early adopter, you earn street credibility and usually get more leeway when you want to try new things. It takes risk to be an early adopter and a bit of self-confidence (or a better word, swagger).

Jamie was an early adopter to an inorganic growth movement at a firm. Jamie and his like-minded peers transformed how this particular company would grow not for the next five years but for the rest of the time the company is in existence. Many people have a fear of early adoption because of the risk. That's okay if you choose to adopt soon after success is found. Better still, you would be better served if you put your fear to the side and became an early adopter with a peer at your company.

### 2. Willingness to change

It is pretty easy to keep doing things the way they have always been done. Using that strategy is low risk because it's "How we do things." Most people who are not willing to change stay in the "average" bucket. The first-quintile salespeople don't like being *average*.

Many leaders I have worked with in the past are willing to change things before their peers do. That doesn't necessarily mean being an early adopter to a new strategic vision, but it means showing a willingness to change a process or system to make it better for the individual and the company. As an example, Jaime was one of the first leaders to have a comprehensive first-meeting packet prepared for his prospects. That led to more second meetings than most people in his firm. It also led to more sales than most people in his firm.

## 3. Desire to win

The desire to win drives many successful people. It's the recognition of being at the top of the rankings or earning the pack of pencils. When you have the desire to win, you are willing to make that extra call and take the extra meeting when you would rather be in bed reading a good book.

## 4. Willingness to work really hard

The standard of "working hard" means different things for everyone. The average performer works the average number of hours and so gets the average amount of results, pay, and recognition. The rock stars work to find efficiency and scale while trying to find balance.

I was interviewing a twenty-something for a job, and he asked me about work and life balance. I stared at the kid and asked him what he meant. He then proceeded to tell me how important his life away from any job is, and as a young person he wanted to have balance in his life. The interview ended, and he went on his merry way. Work/life balance is very important, but I would caution the positioning in an interview. We can all work more efficiently to free up time for things that are important to us away from work.

## 5. Willingness to believe

It probably is not a great strategy to believe whatever you are told, but if you believe what you are told from an expert who has delivered on concepts in the past, you lessen your risk. If you listen to the expert, you then earn the right to double back to the expert to ask questions and test ideas. The concept of dipping your toe in the pool versus jumping in the pool is true. The rock stars test an idea and make a decision to jump in the pool—they simply jump in quicker.

## 6. Willingness to try new things

Some people are uncomfortable about trying new things. It is easy to see because trying new things provides an element of risk. Not many want to take on risk for no reason. That said, the way to supercharge your sales is to do things differently and that usually translates into trying new things. If they work, terrific; if they don't work, toss them in the trash, remember the lesson, and move on.

## 7. Desire to work efficiently

If you choose to work sixty-five hours a week, make sure those hours are the most efficient and effective hours you can put in. Besides your intellectual capital, your time is more precious than gold. Rock stars try to eliminate wasted time. If there isn't a client lunch, they are done eating in fifteen minutes so that they can do something more efficient with their time.

Working efficiently also means leveraging your team and every possible corporate resource to win. As you saw with Frank, the ability to leverage and recognize the team allows you to sell significantly more than the person with a chip on his or her shoulder who says, "I can do this on my own."

## 8. Willingness to ask for help

Smart salespeople realize that it really does take a team effort. By asking for help, they show their intelligence, not their weakness, because they sell more when they leverage other people's talents. Most of my examples in this book are experts in asking for help; they will call on anyone, at any time, to ask for help. It is one of their greatest strengths. They don't ask others to do the work for them; they ask others to help in areas that can create leverage and scale. None of them would want you to fish for them; they want to fish for themselves and then figure out how to have others help them catch more fish.

## 9. Ability to take a punch

As an early adopter, you learn new things along the way. In fact, you blaze a trail for your company. The company learns a lot with a new process, product, or service. You have to be willing to take the punch—in other words, to fail, get up, and try again. When things don't work out, there are some negative ripples that may occur from other parts of the organization; that is a natural response and should be anticipated. Be prepared for the negative response with a thoughtful, fact-based approach to why you did what you did. Others may not agree, but if you lay out your strategic and then tactical action steps, they will appreciate that you made your decisions in a thoughtful way.

## 10. Willingness to evolve

If something's not working, Jamie is willing to change. He wants to and will use whatever is working for his peers, tailoring it to his personality. He is accepting of the fact that he doesn't have all the answers.

## Activity

1.  Are you prepared for yes at the first meeting? If the answer is no, write down what you need to prepare and then put together your resources.

2.  If you are new to a role, spend time with a veteran salesperson to anticipate questions, concerns, or objections you may face. Write them down and practice your responses in front of a mirror.

3.  After looking at the traits of Jamie and others, which ones do you have, and which ones would you like to work on? Write down two you would like to have and remind yourself of those two traits daily. Maybe put a Post-It note on your desk as a memory jog.

# CRM and Data Mining

Data mining may seem a bland or unimportant topic. It is not. Data mining and how you use data will allow you to become more productive and process-oriented, and it will allow you to sell more. If you think data and data mining are boring, think about the fortunes created by those little search engines you use every day. Ten years ago you didn't know you needed Google; now you can't live without it or one of its competitors. You are not Google, but the data you uncover will increase your efficiency, allow you to be more informed in your client's eyes, and help you to make better decisions for the benefit of your clients. Leveraging a CRM and the data that you generate increases your productivity to help you increase your sales.

Most firms have systems and software to keep employees organized and to track information. If your firm does not have a comprehensive, integrated approach to data collection and data mining, now is the time to pay a visit to your boss and begin the influencing process that will drive your firm's productivity.

If you happen to be someone who still lives with a cluttered yellow legal pad, please make a commitment to stop. Contact management platforms exist to help you become more efficient. They make you look smarter as you pull up details of a conversation that you had with a prospect ninety days ago.

CRM is an abbreviation for customer relationship management. Using a CRM keeps things organized and up to date, and it helps you to increase productivity. Salesforce, according to their website in 2014, says that their customers experience a 29 percent increase in sales, a 34 percent increase in sales productivity, and a 42 percent increase in forecast accuracy. I am not sure if every CRM has these results, but what I do know is that you don't get those results from a yellow legal pad or rooting around your trunk trying to find notes from a meeting three months ago.

Let's be skeptical and say the Salesforce numbers are only half right. Will your legal pad help you have even a 15 percent increase in sales? I thought not. Your firm may have an awesome CRM system, but you may be a poser. You intellectually understand the reason you should use the system, but you are not fully committed. You get around to updating it when you can because you are so darn busy. Now is the time to change your habits. Unless you embrace the concept and leverage the power of your CRM, you won't reap the results that you deserve.

## How CRM Helps You

*Target prospects.* With most CRMs, you can load prospect lists that allow you to slice and dice the data for different attributes. These lists are typically refreshed twice a year and allow you to approach prospects with surgical precision. There is always a point person who makes the decisions on data vendors. These people are very important. Invest time with them so that they understand what you are looking for in the data. "Hannah, your role as the keeper of our CRM is critical. When I look at the data, we have just about everything, but I was wondering if you can look into getting more specific ages for our prospects. This will help me to better establish my drip emailing campaigns and drive more people to our succession tool."

*Match appropriate marketing material to a prospects situation.* Tailored marketing, like the specific lure approach I discussed, is the most effective way to get attention. As an example, your CRM allows you to target females over the age of fifty and to send soft copies of information that would interest that demographic. This is also where you can get client-approved material sent to your COI network.

JOHN RICHARD PIERCE JR.

Treating your COIs as a valued client by sending them information you believe is important will help you with referrals. If they don't think the material is of value, they will simply delete it, but they will remember you thought of them.

*View results against your goals in many different formats and time periods.* A valued CRM allows you to target every aspect of your diversified sourcing strategy and helps to ensure that you are hitting all segments. You can then use data generated to see what is the most effective and efficient approach for each of your targeted segments. As an example, you can see how many cold calls you have made, as well as new first meetings, total meetings, employee referrals, COI referrals, offers, or home office visits. You can then compare the data versus a prior period to see where you excel and where you have gaps. This information provides valuable trends. Rock star salespeople always know where their trends are and course correct where necessary.

*Access competitive information shared by colleagues.* Many times firms will establish a shared drive that can be accessed by many people in the organization. This is the perfect vehicle to check on competitive intelligence, updates, and success stories, and to overcome objections. Many times people visit a CI library once and then move on. Often the keeper of the CRM has someone on her or his team updating CI as it comes in from sales calls and more. If that is not happening in your company, pitch in and get the initiative started. If it is happening in your company, make sure you visit the content library once a week and share any learnings with your accountability partner.

*Create follow-up tasks that generate reminders.* After a meeting, you may promise to deliver something to your prospects or schedule a follow-up call. Your CRM allows you to preset everything you need; this keeps you organized and effective. It also makes you look very smart to clients and prospects. "Erin, at our last meeting we agreed that I would call you today after the close of business. Let's go over some new information that I believe will help you and your family."

*Set automatic e-mail touches or other corporate-generated material.* Automatic e-mail is amazing. Your client or prospect believes you are thinking of them when they receive a personalized e-mail from you. Content may not matter; what matters is that you took the time to send them something. It's easy to delete, but the effort will be remembered. Many data vendors do not provide personal e-mail addresses. As discussed, it may be inappropriate to send things to a corporate address.

Before you end any call, check your CRM, and if you don't have a personal e-mail address, ask for it.

*View the effectiveness of materials sent like e-mail open rates and unsubscribe percentages.* It is a wonderful learning experience to use metrics to become more effective. You may have a topic that has unbelievable open rates. When you see that, you can expand the scope of who receives the topic to help you to be more effective. The converse is also true: some topics just don't work, and so you learn to avoid the topic. As an example, some prospects may be very interested in identity theft. If you see high open rates for that topic versus other material, you may expand who receives this e-mail in an attempt to help them and to eventually sell more.

*Provide memory jogs on past conversations.* You are too busy to remember what you had for lunch, let alone the salient contents of a face-to-face meeting ninety days ago. Pull up your notes and refresh your memory before the next conversation or meeting. You look smart, and you are smart because you are leveraging technology to show you care about your client or prospect.

*Understand your metrics.* How are you performing against your peers across the country? Most CRMs have data-aggregation tools that can populate preset performance reporting to look at not only activity but effectiveness. Most CRMs are responsible for the stack rankings that a company publishes or the metrics that are compared between you and your peers.

Safety Tip: Please ensure that your data is accurate. If you put in bad, misrepresented, or inaccurate data, you are hurting yourself in the long run. Your personal data may look awesome, but you are at the bottom of the stack rank. One day someone will say you have either an effectiveness problem or an integrity problem. Like understanding the math, understanding your metrics can show your weak spots, and you can take corrective action. Or the metrics may highlight that you are awesome at something, and you thus become the subject matter expert for your company.

To reach your potential, you need to expand beyond instinct and leverage data. You need data to learn, grow, expand, and exploit opportunities. When you start to create your personal database, you need to invest years, not weeks. A valuable database on your prospects, your industry, and your firm allows you have a pipeline of positive surprises.

The use of data as you develop relationships allows you to get to yes. If you are a pretender in using your CRM, now is the time to change.

## Vocabulary

Salesforce.com: a global cloud computing company headquartered in San Francisco, California

Customer relationship management: a model for managing a company's interactions with current and future customers. It involves using technology to organize, automate, and synchronize sales, marketing, customer service, and technical support

## Activity

Use your CRM daily so it that is as normal as brushing your teeth each morning.

Stop using paper and put everything in your CRM that usually has a cloud backup, so that your life's work is safe and sound.

Don't use the excuse that your CRM is too time consuming. Make your personal investment in the system daily, and you will increase your productivity and therefore sell more.

# Quick Hits III

## The Quick Cut

One of the toughest things to do is cut your losses. You have invested so much time, talent, and treasure in a specific prospect, and you just don't want to give up. You reflect on all the preparation, presentations, overcoming objections, and sweat you have poured into a client or prospect, and you want to keep pushing to try to get to yes. Given how much you have poured into the client or prospect, the prospect has to eventually say yes, right?

Unfortunately, that's not true. A lesson you have already learned or will learn one day is that you can't fall in love with your prospect pipe. You may feel like you have a huge pipe of prospects and opportunities, but if you don't cull your pipe, you will mistake activity for effectiveness. Then your income decreases.

Let's discuss a cautionary tale. Jose was a very high-activity leader on paper. He had constant breakfasts, lunches, and dinners with prospects. He devoted the hours going out on weekends with prospects who became friends. Jose was the guy who always talked in groups about how busy he was and how hard he was working. Jose didn't evolve as his company evolved. He kept doing the same things over and over again, expecting a different outcome. I believe Albert Einstein said that was the definition of insanity.

Eventually the company implemented more robust data-mining and data-capture tools that allowed the company to gather, compare, and examine the activity and effectiveness of all salespeople. Although Jose really was busy—his travel and entertainment reports showed that—it was low-effective activity. Jose would see the same set of prospects eight, nine, or ten times. Jose was busy, but at the end of each quarter he was a fifth-quintile performer. He made the mistake of falling in love with his core set of prospects and never cut the dead wood. He was complacent until he was about to lose his job.

Here are a few safety tips.

Don't fall in love with your prospect pipe.

Your prospect pipe is a number. History has shown that in most industries any pipe over a hundred people is probably too large. Many of the wealth management firms say the optimal number of clients is one hundred meaningful clients, which allows you to implement a robust client-service model that creates referrals and greater productivity and profitability. In the wealth management model, you may have some awesome clients who don't do any business, or you may have some clients with a lot of money but who are a drain on your support system and don't do a lot of business.

Take the time and rank your prospect and client pipe as a one, two, three, or four. What you base it on is up to you. If you have existing clients, maybe you base it on historical sales. You may find that 80 percent of your sales are from the ones and twos. If that is the case, the threes and fours could be resource drains for you; you should either cut them or develop a game plan to increase sales.

If your prospect list has people whom you have met with three times or more face-to-face, it may be time to cut the prospect from your active pipe. Depending on a sales cycle, this can turn out to be a judgment call based on you or your colleague's experience. The key is to understand why the sales process has not advanced and make a decision around your level of effort with the prospect. Have a conversation with them. "Jim, I really enjoy our time together. Unfortunately, we only have so many hours in the day. Unless I can get a better sense of why we have not done business together after the last eight months, we probably should stop the frequent contact.

What can I do to earn your business?" Everyone should be on your automated drip e-mail list, but stop the resource drain if you are not making progress.

Don't waste time with existing clients who won't do what you believe is in their best interest. Tell them you are disappointed they won't heed your advice and guidance, and let them know that contact will be diminished and that the steak dinners are finished. If people will not listen to you, you might also consider giving that client to someone else at your company. If clients won't listen to you, are they worth your time? If clients won't listen to you, do you increase any personal risk if they complain about you?

Stop pretending that there is a diamond in a pipe that should not be cut. There is not. There are a multitude of other prospects to whom you can sell. The story of Jose is clear. You need new blood in your pipeline. You need to see new prospects every week. You need to develop relationships with other people.

Take the action step of evaluating your prospect and client pipe. Maybe a client does not do a lot of business with you but is a referral machine. Don't throw your head out the window—that person is a one.

A fun exercise to do is spending time with your support team, which tends to deal with a lot of your clients and prospects. Ask them who they would cut and why. You will have some eye-opening, fact-based conversations that will help your business if you choose to act on it.

When you know someone is not a fit for what you do, end it quickly. "Tim, based on how you run your business and what your needs are, it's clear to me that we are not a good fit for you at this time. I would like to know more people like you who do business a little differently, so if you have any suggestions of people I should contact, I would appreciate that. I wish you nothing but success in the future."

It never hurts to ask for a referral when you are gently letting down someone. You may not get a lot of referrals, but every once in a while you will. Think of the referral ask as payment to you for all the time you or your team spent with them.

Many of the leaders in this book are good at culling their pipes and moving on. They know that their most valuable asset is their personal time. By cutting low-quality prospects, you have the ability to add new high-quality opportunities. Spending time with people who are not buyers is not a prospect—it is a drain of your time. Cut them and replace them with real prospects with whom you can develop a relationship.

Do yourself a favor: cut poor prospects and move on to the next yes.

**Activity**

Candidly review your list of clients and prospects for people you should stop working with or stop prospecting.

Create your list and discuss it with anyone who helps you with your sales process.

Get rid of the problem client and stop prospecting people who are wasting your time or are not a good fit.

It is also important, though difficult, that you do the same with people on your team.

## Change

Things change, and you need to change as well. View change as an opportunity to become better and to help more people. View change as an opportunity to sell more.

In every organization I see unbelievably talented people get fired or stuck in the same job because they didn't change or evolve. They figured they were high performers and didn't need to change. They figured they had enough institutional history and had built up enough credibility to survive. Then the world changed. We need to be aware of when our world is changing and make sound decisions on what to do next.

Please accept a few core tenets.

- Change happens whether or not we agree with it
- Seek to understand why things changed
- Accept that if we refuse to change, we have the potential of putting our job in danger
- Before you make the decision to change, look in the mirror and accept the change, make the decision to try to influence the change, or decline to accept the change—those are your three key options

If you accept that change is inevitable, you have to truly embrace the change and not just pretend to embrace the change. Pretenders may get away for a year, but after that they are found out and lose a year adapting to the change, and their peers will be well ahead of them.

If you want to attempt to modify the change, you really need to understand why the change happened, who was the driver of that change, and why. Then in a fact-based manner, lay out why the change may not be the most optimal for your firm. If your fact-based argument does not work, you now have two decisions: accept or decline the change. It may be in your best interest to decline the change and move on. If the change is going to make you miserable, what is the point?

Many of us do things the way we like to do them. We are comfortable doing it the way we like. Change is hard and can be scary. Change can also be transformational and extend our careers for many years. Instead of potentially overreacting to change, take some think time and work through what the change means to you and your significant others. Spend time with your accountability partner to make sure you have a good grasp of the change.

## Activity

Are there things that you know you "should do" or have been "highly encouraged" to do by your company, but you avoid adopting them? Please write them down.

Consider understanding why people want you to change and then consider changing. I changed to a smartphone recently, and although my friends made fun of me when I was learning how to use it, I am more productive today. I should have changed a few years ago but resisted.

Consider changing what you wrote down.

# The Grand Shortcut

### Four Words: There Are No Shortcuts

A large part of this book covers the concepts of your personal responsibility, sweat effort, process improvement, innovation, attitude, and swagger. Every firm has a swath of poorly performing salespeople. You will always have a fifth quintile. If your firm is typical, your first quintile delivers 80 percent of your results. That 20 percent probably embodies many of the concepts in this book.

The fifth quintile's sales are not where they need to be. Here is the place where you find the most people who believe these three words: "There are shortcuts."

Pretenders can look like star performers for a short sequence. That is why most leaders don't pat the star on the back too often until there is sustained, repeatable success. What happens with the short-cutters is that they do something that works as a shortcut but that it isn't repeatable. They end the year in the first-quintile bucket, and then the next year they are in the fifth quintile or in the middle of the pack.

The short-cutters will blame everyone but the person in the mirror for their personal performance.

Can a fifth-quintile person become a first-quintile person? Yes. That occurrence is very rare, but it does happen.

It starts:

- With the person in the mirror
- Making a decision to change
- Making a decision to put in the sweat equity
- Making a decision to ask for help
- Making a decision to take responsibility
- Making a decision to keep going even when things are not working

Unfortunately, most leaders learn over time that a fifth quintile is there for a reason. That person does not make the effort and does not do what is listed above. The leader realizes she or he can't do the job for that person. Once the leader realizes this, the care, feeding, and watering of that person diminishes.

The leader realizes the people he or she needs to care, feed, and water are the first quintilers and the high-activity, low-effectiveness people who want to get better. Many of you learned the lesson the same way I did. I wanted everyone to succeed. I could see the dramatic, positive impact a person could have on his or her family, and so I tried hard to help. Then I realized I had more passion for some people's success than they had. It is a difficult, painful lesson to learn. Performers are not wired to be mediocre. Performers don't understand why other people can't see how awesome something can be.

Once you realize you want success more than the person you are trying to help, you have to let it go. You have to focus on people who want to win. You have to agree that you will not fish for that person. If you believe there are *shortcuts*, please throw this book away.

## Activity

Although it may be difficult, self-assess if you have taken any shortcuts recently, specifically in the review of your diversified sourcing strategy. Please write the shortcut down. If you have taken a shortcut or two, course correct and refrain from that shortcut in the future.

If you have decided to shortcut the math, admit it, write it down, and get back to the math on a daily basis.

# Short-Term Thinking

You have built the foundation that a sale needs to be good for your client or prospect, your company, and finally you. Many times we can be tempted into making a quick sale when we know it may not be in the best interest of the client. When you do that, you tend to have regret. If you have regret, eventually your client may have regret, and that can set off a cascade of negative ripples. Besides not getting any additional referrals, you may have returns that lead to claw backs of your compensation. If your clients are dissatisfied, not only will they not purchase more from you, but they spread negative word of mouth that hurts your and your company's reputations. In addition, making a bad sale or hiring someone who you know is not a fit can harm a culture that took years to establish.

Too often we have a short-term horizon that may add a lot of alpha but leaves a trail of scorched earth behind. You probably know a person who is high productivity for short bursts but tends to change jobs frequently. You see his or her resume after ten years, and as a leader you know he or she is not a long-term fit anywhere. It is really unfortunate that people will change jobs so often. As you interview people, you will see the perfect candidate, and then you dig into the resume, and he or she has a short-term job change pattern. The simple question is what will change at your company to break an eighteen-month cycle? You don't want to invest your sweat, equity, or intellectual capital on an eighteen-month employee even if she or he adds a lot of alpha.

As a side note, there is an amazing financial services leader named Bob who told me that no job you have counts unless you have been in it for two years. Bob's point was simple and elegant: it takes time to learn a job and then to become proficient in that job. Two years is a minimum, not the time to move again. Too many young people change jobs for a couple of thousand dollars more, and when they get to the point of interviewing for a more meaningful job, the eighteen-month syndrome takes them off the short list of potential candidates. Think of your jobs in five-year chunks, not eighteen-month chunks.

## A Personal Case Study on Negative Self-Talk

I would like to share a personal story around a concept that occurs in business, in daily life, and in personal interactions. The concept is negative self-talk. These are the thoughts that circulate in your brain at times and can get you off track and away from what you want to accomplish. I am going to explain two different concepts to eliminate this negativity.

Here is my personal example. In the summer of 2014, I had been preparing for a long-distance triathlon. Physically I was prepared, but mentally I was not at the peak of my performance ability. Because I was not as prepared as I needed to be, the negative thoughts in my mind spiraled out of control during the race, and I ended up having a horrible day.

I didn't do the two things I needed to do to overcome my bad day.

## I. Become Aware

On this day, I never got to the point where I was aware I was having negative self-talk. Things kept piling on, and negative thoughts piled on more negativity. Usually if you are making a presentation or doing an activity, there is a little voice in the back of your head that says, "This is not going as well as expected—time to change something." You may find that when you have negative self-talk, there tends to be a piling-on effect. In my example, the swim in my race was not wetsuit legal, so I swam without equipment I was used to. At the time I was fifty years old, so my starting wave was at the end of the queue, and I had to swim against an incoming current for the majority of the race. In addition, the week before I had my bike checked out and found out I had a crack in my bike frame. There was little chance it would break, but it was still there. I got out of the swim, and I didn't see my wife, which was odd based on past races, and I started a long and windy bike ride wondering about her and the crack in my bike frame.

What you will find is that as all these little negatives swirl in your mind, you tend to exaggerate things. About sixty miles into my ride I still hadn't seen my wife, and I was worried something was wrong at home and she had left. I had absolutely no reason to think that, but that was my frame of mind at that moment. I was not positive, and I was not productive.

Because I had so many negative thoughts in my mind, I never got to the point where I was aware of the impact on my race. Had I become aware, I could have acted to change the negative self-talk. My first piece of advice is to mentally pause when you have negative thoughts in anything you do. Become aware that these negative thoughts will impact your performance.

I found out after the race that my wife simply got stuck in bad traffic. There was nothing wrong at home. My swim was slow, but so was everyone else's. My bike frame was cracked, but it didn't break. My exaggerated negative self-talk was just an illusion that added no positive value and hurt my performance.

## II. Act and Compartmentalize

In this example, I never got to the point I usually get to: action. Once you become aware of negative thoughts and feelings, you need to deal with them.

Here are the three things I tend to do to act and compartmentalize.

1. I think about how awesome each of my kids are, and what great experiences they have had in life. I start with Meghan and then go to John and then Thomas. Then I think some more about Thomas, then John, and then Meghan. By the time I get through two cycles, I am smiling about something. Find something close to your heart that can make you smile when you have negative self-talk.

2. Other times I will repeat a mantra. I may say a bunch of Hail Marys back to back to get into a mental groove. I find that repeating a mantra can bring a sense of calm and peace. When you calm down, you think more rationally, and the negative spiral is minimized.

3. In this example, if nothing else is working, I count telephone poles. Yes, telephone poles. I start at zero and count to fifty and then count back from fifty to zero. By the time I count one hundred telephone poles, my mind is so bored that I forget about all the other stuff.

I realize you can't count telephone poles during a presentation, but you can pause and take a sip of water and have a brief reflection about what makes you happy to get back on track. A five- to ten-second pause in a presentation may seem like a long time internally, but if it gets you back on track, there is no harm. If nothing else, smile about telephone poles, get back to your written talking points, and try to have a little fun!

Whenever you have negative self-talk circling around your brain, attempt to recognize it, act to minimize it, and then compartmentalize it.

## Activity

1. Reflect on past times when things didn't go as well as you wanted. Was there any negative self-talk involved? If you can think of examples, write them down and reflect on what you could have done differently.
2. In your day-to-day activities attempt to become self-aware when negativity creeps into your brain. Act and dissipate that negativity.

## The Pivot

The pivot refers to your *flexibility*. I talked earlier about not taking anything personally or overreacting; this is a little different. Unless you master the pivot, you may end up frustrated and disappointed.

The *pivot* refers to:

- Your nimbleness when you are not making any headway with the prospect.

  Fall back on "I'm really seeking to understand where we are in the process, because we seem to be stalled."

- Your ability to react, as discussed earlier.

  Always pause and take stock of any new information. It is appropriate and smart to repeat back what was said to ensure that you accurately heard what the prospect said. What you don't want to do is freeze up or react negatively.

- Your ability to turn a mistake into an opportunity.

  As you go through the sales process, problems happen. Instead of blaming the company or your team, own up to the issue and take personal responsibility. Discuss with your prospect why the problem happened, what you are going to do personally to rectify it, and what you are going to do to ensure that the problem does not happen again. Even if you had nothing to do with the problem, take responsibility and attempt to get positive closure.

- Your ability to take new information that you may feel blindsided by, and to keep the sales process moving to yes.

  You learn that a competitor has completely undercut your price, and you were unaware of that competitor's push in your territory. Don't throw up your hands and move on to the next prospect. Seek to understand the new pricing in greater detail. Oftentimes new pricing hides back-end charges, exit fees, or fees that are not fully disclosed. In addition, if the price is too good to be true, it probably is too good to be true, and you need to explore that with your prospect. "Wow, that price is well below industry standards. I'm not sure this is an apples-to-apples comparison. If we went that low, we could not stay in business." It is fair to interject doubt on a topic if you have a hard time believing it. It is also an opportunity to gather more CI on the price sensitivity of a particular prospect.

As you seek to understand when you are surprised by something, avoid the temptation to make negative comments about a competitor. Many times you may be faced with a competitor, and their solution looks too good to be true. The headline gets everyone's attention, but you need to read about the details to understand the true situation. The headline is the eye-catching optics, and the details are not seen at first. You can position the concept of optics. "The optics on that pricing just seem off. I'd like to understand the nuances of the pricing to ensure that you are not assuming you are getting one price when the total price to you may be substantially different."

Remember, you want your prospects to come to you because of the value you deliver. If they come to you for what you can deliver, they will forget their past relationships. Even if a firm is shooting itself in the foot, don't pile on. "Yes, I saw that company Y is having some very difficult technology issues. I'm sure they will figure it out over time. Let's refocus on how we can help you right now and in the future."

First embrace the fact that any sale is not a straight-line process. A friend named Brian shows a windy road in a presentation he gives. He talks about the need to stay on the road, and, more importantly, the road has twists and turns that he will drive on together with the client. The more complex the sale, the longer the road to yes. That road happens to be full of toll booths, rest stops, and mountains.

The pivot is not just about overcoming objections. It's taking the conversation and relationship in a completely different direction as needed. Many times the pivot involves dropping the entire sales process and sharing a common experience. You may learn that a prospect enjoys art. Your local art museum probably does tours of little-known facts of a museum, or maybe a docent has a program of hidden treasures that people miss. Take your prospect to an event like that and don't even discuss your company, your business, or selling anything. When the event is over, send the hand-written note with a real stamp letting the prospect know how much you enjoyed your time together. In a few weeks schedule a meeting focused on selling more, now that there is a deeper, nonbusiness connection.

No company or industry is perfect. In the financial services business, it seems like there is a crisis or event every five to seven years. The pivot may be addressing the lack of trust created by your company or the industry. Whatever the issue, be fact-based and honest, and provide your personal views and beliefs. These views and beliefs may not follow the company script, but that's okay; you need to be genuine and honest. Clients and prospects appreciate your honesty, and they will stay with you longer because you exhibit that trait. As discussed earlier, retention of your existing clients is one of your key objectives each and every day.

Many times pivots are about you opening up personally when you are at a log jam. Having a prospect understand how much you believe that you can help her or his family (again, it must be genuine and authentic).

The truth is a great pivot point. To be clear, I believe you have to tell the truth all the time. Telling the truth all the time also avoids the need to remember misrepresentations. Did you tell Tom this and Nedra that, or did you tell Nedra that and Tom something else? "Matt, I really don't understand why we keep going over the same topic on your perception of our company. I must have completely missed your passion on the subject, and for that I am truly sorry. I believe in my heart that I can help you. I need you to help me understand what I am missing here." Taking off the corporate armor and showing your authentic self is not only honest, but it helps to develop long-lasting relationships that lead to repeat sales. Your authentic self also allows you to retain clients longer, and with retention comes deeper relationships and greater referrals. It also helps you to get a good night's sleep when you have done your best in the most honest way, even if you didn't get the sale. The sale will come—maybe not from that prospect, but it will come as you gain a positive reputation in your particular marketplace. When it is time to pivot, pause and think through your options. Be honest. Be genuine. Be authentic. Smile and figure it out!

## Vocabulary

Flexibility: the quality of being able to change or be changed easily according to the situation

Pivot: a fixed point supporting something which turns or balances, or a person or thing on which something else depends

JOHN RICHARD PIERCE JR.

### Activity

List one area where you could pivot today to help develop stronger relationships with your clients or prospects. It may be an area that you are concerned about addressing, or an area that you believe will help people but takes some risk to bring up. Now is the time to pivot on that area.

# PART 7:

## Closing Thoughts

# Case Study: George— Vacation and Exercise

A good friend named George told me, "Johnny, I learned a valuable lesson that I still have to work on, as do you." The lesson was simple: use your vacation.

As George and I talked at the end of a very long year, we were both tired, frayed, and a little bit chippy with everyone. I was about to take the end of the year off, and by coincidence Thanksgiving, Christmas, and the Jewish holidays were in the middle of that time period.

I slept in more over a two-week period than I had in the previous ten years. It was awesome. George's message to me was simple: all the work, problems, and to-dos would still be there when the holidays were over. George was right. All the things I needed to do were still there when I returned. The difference was that I was relaxed, refreshed, and recharged.

I also invested in a lot of think time that helped to form my next career steps.

George also introduced me to *The Four Agreements*, which I reference in the suggested reading section. I have a tendency to take stuff too personally. It's like in the movies when no one else can say anything negative about your friends, but your friends can say anything to each other. Some of the core tenets of the book focus on not taking things personally, doing what you say you will do, being honest in your actions, and not making assumptions. These are terrific lessons from which we can learn.

George has always been a proponent of "seek to understand."

Seeking to understand can be a major building block of your relationship foundation. Seeking to understand, tied to the books I reference later, may help you to relax more and build stronger relationships.

Besides sleeping in, I worked out like a maniac on this particular vacation. I took really long runs in winter conditions, I did long spins on a trainer while watching movies I'd missed that year, and I hit the pool for some easy yardage. I've found—and you may have as well—that a long run in the elements allows quality think time. I don't run with headphones and music blaring; besides being a distraction, that doesn't allow me to observe the external environment, and I usually don't let my mind wander when I am listening to music.

Safety Tip: Please keep the volume down or run with just one ear bud in, if you choose to listen to music. It's important to be aware of who is around you at all times. Meghan, my daughter, might say "Oh Dad," but it is advice I trust.

Some of my best ideas appear when I'm alone working out or near the brink of exhaustion when my mind is not focused. Then an idea pops up, and I smile. If it happens to you, write it down and then think about that idea. For you, it may not be exercise. You may unwind at art museums, walking through parks, going to a library, volunteering, or something else you really enjoy. The point is that you need to escape the grind. Many companies let you accrue sick time, but who uses all that? Although many companies don't eliminate accrued sick time, they do delete your vacation time. All of us would be better off if we took the time off we earned.

### Activity

Start acting on George's three-pronged advice:
Seek to understand the next time you don't get it.
Use your vacation; plan your next week off today.
Work out or enjoy your particular passion this week.

# Reconnect with People

Every industry is small. If you have been working ten to fifteen years in any industry, you realize this fact. Too often we keep our heads down and work our tails off, and then next thing we know, five years have passed, and we think, "How did that happen?"

It is important to take your institutional blinders off and stay connected with people who have meaning to you. You will change jobs and move to a different location. You will move up or down the food chain. Try to stay connected. This is important as you prepare for the certainty that your life will change, because the change may not happen according to your ten-year plan.

While growing in an industry, you have opportunities to do new things within a company. A person may decide to be a producer for an entire career, have a terrific experience, and create multigenerational wealth. Others may decide to go corporate and see how far up the ladder they can advance. As the years pass, new people join the organization from competitors in different roles, and friends and colleagues leave the firm to join other competitors. This is where you need to keep your personal addresses and phone numbers up to date and connect with people as they transition.

Usually a shock hits every industry every five to ten years. Other shocks are created by one industry that affects others. In 2008–2009 the financial services industry caused a global shock led by greed and hubris, with the sale of mortgages to many people who probably should not have owned a home. This debt, at times inappropriately repackaged, sliced, diced, and sold off, caused years of pain across every segment of our world population. As shocks like these happen, stay in touch with people who leave the industry or are displaced. They may one day return the favor to you when it really matters.

Some shocks are success shocks—for example, the variable annuity example we discussed earlier. Life insurance firms sold too much, and the end result was the termination of all the top sales people. When shocks occur, many firms use the event as an excuse to "right size" their employment force. It happens every cycle. Sales increase, the head count gets bloated, and when the finance or human resources people analyze the numbers, they slash bodies and expenses in anticipation of weaker times. These examples will continue to happen for as long as you live. You need to stay connected with people as they change jobs, firms, or locations. You need to prepare for the certainty of some change in your life. As you go along in your job, take the time to gather personal information (home phone numbers, personal e-mail addresses, and home addresses) of people who leave. This is also why you should stay connected via LinkedIn.

I left a firm once, and a person I thought was a friend wouldn't return my calls or speak with me after I left. I was dumbfounded. We had taken vacations together and spoke all the time. Years passed, and the firm he worked at does not exist in the form it was in its glory days. He now works at a competitor. Don't be afraid to stay in touch with people if a friend goes to your fiercest competitor. Your company has no say in who your friends are.

By now you know this book's foundation is based on relationships, not what company you work for today. If you have friends or colleagues who matter to you, make the effort to stay in touch, especially if they are rocked by an internal or external shock. Even though you may not be able to help them today, the nice note or call of concern matters.

If you choose to stay in touch, be genuine. It takes effort. Keep a list of influential people and periodically reach out to them just to say hello. I also recommend that you back all your collected data up on the cloud with a service like *Dropbox*. If you lose your company phone or your contacts, it can be very difficult to replicate. As you think about influential people and connect with them, they will think about you as they go through their lives as well. That's when opportunity blossoms. Connections are made, and people think about you when they see an opportunity. As you expand your network, you will stay in touch with more people and will potentially sell more as well.

If you have not done a good job staying in touch with former colleagues, start today. It is not effective to call your "friends" whom you haven't spoken with in three years and say, "Hey, buddy, I'm looking for a new role. Can you help?"

Spend some time thinking about all the people with whom you used to be in touch. List them in your database and start connecting, one person at a time. I suggest you start by leveraging social media and then progressing to phone calls and eventually face-to-face meetings. Be brutally honest with them. "I've done a really poor job staying in touch. I picked my head up, and several years have passed. I just wanted to reach out to you and do a better job staying in touch." The honest, genuine approach is the most effective way to get reconnected.

You may think you are at your last company, your last stop, and so you pour all your energy into this endeavor. Don't fall into that trap. Having a network of friends and colleagues from your past may be your ticket to a much brighter future. Be organized and genuine in your approach. As the sands of time pass, you will be prepared for the unexpected, and you will be happier staying in touch with people you like!

## Vocabulary

Dropbox: a service that lets you bring your photos, docs, and videos anywhere and share them easily

## Activity

Write down the names of three people who had impact on you in the past, or who were important to you at one time in your life, but with whom you have lost touch. Please call them.

# The End, My Friends ...

This has been a fun journey with you. I can't be sure how much you will change or how much your sales will grow after reading this book. You really have to change some things if you want to have transformational growth. The choice seems easy, but now that you see the list of stuff to do, it may seem daunting. Don't let it be daunting. You know the best way to eat an elephant? Yes, in small bites, one bite at a time. Maybe you will consider stack ranking where you are really deficient and start improving bite by bite. Maybe you stack rank where you are awesome and start sharing that bite by bite.

I wrote this book with some very specific tactical action steps. Over the past twenty years, I have seen some awesome leaders implement all this stuff. All the leaders in this book have been knocked down, skinned their knees, broken their noses, and bled on the floor. Instead of giving up, they stood up and changed to make a difference. Some may say the specific tactical action steps are too defined and to scripted. Nonsense. I'm tired of reading books that have a high-concept strategy focus, and you are left with nothing that is time-tested or proven to work.

Building relationships is the core tenet to selling more. You have to buy into that concept, and then you have to implement the tactics. Now that we are finished, you have to choose to act. Please don't close the book and move on. Please act on some of the lessons learned in this book. You will sell more, and you will sell the right way. When you sell more the right way, you can lay your head on your pillow and have an awesome sleep.

I end where I began. Thank you for purchasing this book.

*John*

Post Script: Please purchase an additional copy of this book for a friend or colleague. Think of this small investment as a way to pay it forward in honor of people who have helped you in the past.

# PART 8:

## Bonus Coverage

# Suggested Reading

All three of my kids are voracious readers. If you have kids, buy them books. Their vocabulary will astound you after a few years. When they get into high school and college, their ability to write will dumbfound you. Kids soak up so much when they read. All three of my kids are superior writers compared to me, and I believe it started with their love of reading. The Internet is not going away. However, please make sure your kids and loved ones get to read some great books and remember the feel of turning the actual pages and not swiping the screen. The quietest our home has ever been was during the Harry Potter years. By book three we ran to a local bookstore and purchased three copies each time it was published. The house was silent for the next day. Reading can be magical.

Here are a few books that I would suggest you consider reading. We need books like these to expand our minds and learn new stuff. I trust you have your own personal favorites list, and they will be completely different from mine. That's what makes this country so awesome: we get to choose what's special to each of us.

- *Atlas Shrugged,* by Ayn Rand. My dad gave me this book, and it is one of the few books I have ever reread.
- *The Art of War,* by Sun Tzu
- *Animal Farm,* by George Orwell
- *Lord of the Flies,* by William Golding
- *The Four Agreements,* by Don Miguel Ruiz
- The Declaration of Independence

- *Business Etiquette in Brief,* by Ann Marie Sabath
- *Becoming a Resonant Leader: Develop Your Emotional Intelligence, Renew Your Relationships, Sustain Your Effectiveness,* by Richard Boyatzis, Annie McKee, and Frances Johnston

## Activity

Write down a book that you would to read.

Commit to buying it this week.

Read twenty pages of that first book within forty-eight hours of purchase, and be on your way to learning something new and having some pleasure reading!

# If You Lead Teams

## Case Study: Darin—The Entrepreneur

The focus of this section revolves around the need to try new things, to expand your comfort zone, and to accept risk as a way to increase your sales and deepen your relationships. To better understand these concepts, I would like to spend some time on a case study of Darin. Darin is an *entrepreneur*. He leads a company that helps other companies with a segment of a diversified sourcing strategy. Over the years I have learned a lot from Darin. Darin is a classic leader who is willing to try new things, fail, and then go right back to trying new things. Sometimes a new idea or concept will work out; other times it will not. The beauty of thinking and acting like an entrepreneur is that it will allow you to discover new opportunities and help your team to be more productive. The entrepreneur inside of you needs to be found if you want to grow your sales or influence others.

When Darin senses an opportunity, he will beta test his idea on a small market. If he gets positive results, he will expand territory and build partnerships with existing clients to mitigate his risk and expenses. Darin is the poster child of ideas that are tried, dropped, tweaked, or implemented. If you have an idea, don't have regrets five years from now—"I wish I would have tried this," or even worse, "That was my idea! This isn't fair!" This has nothing to do with your company's marketing materials or the presence it has in the marketplace. This is about new ideas that could super-charge growth from an entrepreneurial perspective.

Darin is attuned to competitive intelligence and the importance of gathering and understanding what that CI will mean to an industry. He leverages the external environment to help his company and get a step up on his competition. Darin is also very sociable with his competition. When industry events occur, he makes the time to attend. When he is invited to events, he attends even if there is no short-term gain. Darin focuses on the future. Many times you don't want to associate with your competition, and that is a long-term mistake. Even though you have competitors, they go through the same ups and downs as the industry changes and goes through a market cycle. Having the ability to speak and commiserate with a competitor without talking about the specifics of a deal or confidential company information is helpful.

For example, most industry leading companies bring their top salespeople together on a consistent basis. Darin is friendly with his competitors, adds value by asking the hard questions, and wants to learn. Darin realized sometime during his life: learning never stops. Any bit of new knowledge can lead to the next sale, the next relationship, or the next publication in a trade magazine. All of that leads to new sales.

Darin was recently at an event I attended, and he commented, "It is like the last one." This was not a negative comment. It was a fact-based overview. After he said that, he said the following.

- This is terrific because I get to see a different view from other people.
- I get to learn about an area where we don't spend enough time on.
- We learn how other people think about things to help us sell more.
- Please invite me and our team to the next event.

As an optimist, the glass is half full. You have the opportunity to figure out why the glass is half full. It is important to be a half-full kind of person in order to have sustainable long-term relationships, sales, and personal growth. Can a pessimist do well? Yes. My personal belief is that the negative energy that a pessimist creates is not worth the time or the effort. It is hard to be a pessimist. Why do that?

The case study also uncovered five entrepreneurial traits that strong leaders exhibit.

## Entrepreneurial Traits to Adopt

### Willing to take risks

If you are a "play it safe" person, you can do okay in life. The entrepreneurs who take the risk reap the reward. Only in hindsight can someone say, "I wish I would have taken that risk." Entrepreneurs take the risk and pay the price because when it doesn't work out, there can be significant collateral damage. Taking smart, well-thought-out risks can lead to meaningful strategic shifts that a company can adopt. That is very different compared to "have a hunch, bet a bunch."

### Willing to adapt

As a business owner, you deal with a lot of change that can be positive or challenging. As a sales leader, you need to be willing to adapt as the industry changes. You could wake up one day and find that the wonderful environment you used to work in no longer exists. If that happens in your job or your industry, you need to be careful how you react, and then you should adapt with your long-term game plan.

### Persistent and determined

Darin and his team exhibit the drive to get things done in good times and in challenging times. They keep driving forward with the faith that their effort and sweat equity will end up creating more sales. Roadblocks and objections are thought of as nice ways to delay the inevitable yes.

## Loving what you do

If you don't love your job, you will have a hard time exhibiting the other characteristics Darin and his team embody. You never love every aspect of your job, and you never love your job all the time. The key is to love what you do and then work through the other things. Darin loves what he does, and he has fun doing it. Because he lives in Colorado he shuts down his firm during key ski season weeks, and everyone gets to have some fun on the slopes. They come back to work eager, refreshed, and excited to earn the next sale.

## Willing to ride the roller coaster

As you take the punches that life throws at you, you have a choice. Do you stay down on the mat, or do you get up? When you get hit in the face metaphorically, how do you react? Do you learn and avoid the next punch? You can take a little risk and accept that you will probably be punched once in a while. As you get punched, you learn, and as you learn, you end up selling more. Try to avoid the punches that can really hurt. Instead of cutting ties and moving on when confronted with changing news, Darin exhibited many characteristics in this book: patience, seeking to understand, pivot with a change, trust in partners that will lead to more sales.

The most successful salespeople try new things and fail more than they succeed. If you have an idea, write it down; test the pros and cons. This case study was to highlight someone who tries new things and is willing to accept the risk of change. It also ties back to the importance of having a passion for what you do while exhibiting the five entrepreneurial traits discussed.

## Vocabulary

> Entrepreneur: a person who attempts to make a profit by starting a company or by operating alone in the business world, esp. when it involves taking risks

## Activity

It might be helpful for you to reflect on entrepreneurs who you know and consider the traits they exhibit. Can you adopt some of those traits in your business? Second, think about things that you have wanted to change at your company that would mean taking on a little risk. It may be helpful to write these down and spend time weighing the long-term positives of accepting some personal risk to help you and your company.

# Case Study: Manish—Hire Smart

As you think about your sales team, it is important to consistently evaluate who is on the team. Your objective is to have the best team to grow your sales. There are times when you need to change team members or, as you grow, expand the team. Many times you may be hesitant to hire someone because she may be better than you in certain areas. That hesitance or fear is understandable, but you must overcome it. In this section I would like to spend time discussing the important of hiring skilled team members.

A guy I know named Manish is not afraid to hire talent. Why is this important to you? As you have success, you will need to expand your team. As you expand, you need to hire smart. Manish realizes he needs to hire people better than him in areas that will complement the team and help achieve corporate and personal goals. The sad part of this sentence is that you inwardly said, "That makes a ton of sense."

Unfortunately, many people don't think like Manish. They are afraid to hire smarter people with different talents or expertise. They are afraid to hire people who will help the organization. Why? They want the next couple of paychecks. They don't want to look like they don't know what they are doing. They don't want to be threatened. It scares me when I see companies that don't hire external talent or that don't promote internally from different parts of the organization for stretch assignments.

Manish gets it. He understands that he needs to stretch the organization, bring in talent, and challenge the conventional wisdom of "This is how we do things in this company." When you hire talented people, you will break a lot of glass. Manish gets that, because all his type-A hires want to change things yesterday.

To sell more, you need to surround yourself with people better at different things in your organization than you are. This is not just about the corporate sales organization—this is about the team that supports you from start to finish. I have discussed the team concept, and if you have not written down the team members who help you to be successful, you should. After you write the list down, the question becomes where the weak points are.

As you identify weak points, you will need to do more selling—not a product or a service, but the concept that you need to strengthen the team. You will have to do this with your boss, peers, and colleagues because you will most likely not have direct control of every person who helps you to be successful. If there continues to be a gap with shipping of a product versus a competitor, now is the time to find out why. "Is it our people? Is it our process, an external vendor issue, or a combination of many things?" By working with the team that is in charge of shipping, you can help influence solutions and press for higher quality people if that is a gap. If your company is not known for first-class service, that will hurt your repeat sales. You need to influence the team that delivers service so that service becomes a strength and not a gap with your clients. You can learn of your strengths and gaps from your competitors.

Manish is also pretty good about seeing around corners. I discussed Mike and the ripples earlier, and you can equate that to seeing around corners. To be clear, no one can accurately predict the future. That said, if you implement many things in this book, you will get a sense of where the industry is moving. If you capitalize as a first mover, you will sell more before your competition catches up.

To see around corners, you need a really solid understanding of your competition.

- What's happening in the industry?
- Who are the new competitive entrants, and what are they selling?
- What firms have added new stuff to the shelf?
- Talent movement in the industry
  - Always keep track of the rock stars and watch their progress at each firm. Try to hire them when you can.
  - What are the best salespeople in the industry doing, and what are they doing differently from you?
  - Even if you don't have a role on the team, interview as many of your competitors as you can in order to gain CI.
- Who keeps getting all the trade publication press and why?
- What's happening at trade conferences?
- What are industry client surveys saying?
- What are your gaps and advantages of your client surveys? (Don't have a robust client survey? Time to invest in one!)

I understand that there are only so many hours in a day, and you need to prioritize your time because it is the most valuable asset you have. With that said, as you read the tea leaves, you get a sense of what may happen in the industry. If you hire people better than you in a specific area, you are then prepared to execute and have first-mover advantage when something changes. When someone at the competition changes her or his approach and is taking your market share, you will not be pleased with yourself for misjudging the pulse of your industry. Most people don't keep enough attention on their competitors because they are so focused on selling more of their own stuff. That is short-term thinking that leads to long-term mistakes.

Preparing the organization for new things, based on selling more, is preparing for the ripples. Most corporate push back is from people who have no clue how hard it is to generate revenue, start a new revenue line, or do your job. You can't overreact, but you can prepare the organization for change.

As a cautionary tale, don't have a meteoric rise and then revert back to "This is how we do things." Manish is great about constantly pushing an organization to evolve. He knows that the only way to sell more is to evolve and grow. Please don't miss the point as it relates to your sales job. You need to help influence, push, move, drive, and direct things you believe in, in order for you to sell more.

George in the book joined a company, and after a few months he realized there were some glaring product gaps. He created a well-thought-out list of gaps and worked with senior leaders in the organization to fix the gaps. George always seeks to understand, and although three years after he joined some of the original gaps still exist, the company started to realize they could not go up market until the issues identified were fixed. This was frustrating, but George exhibited patience. The moral of the story is that if you do things the right way, gather fact-based data, and work personally and professionally, then you will eventually move the rock up the hill.

In the long term, help your organization hire smarter, and keep a closer pulse on your competition. As you learn more, you will sell more. One of the unintended consequences may be your ability to lure talent to your organization. Another unintended consequence is that you may get the attention of a competitor and be considered for a much larger job. That's not the intent of your networking and CI, but you always have to keep your options open.

## Vocabulary

Ripple effect: a series of things that happen as the result of a particular action or event

### Activity

If you have a team I would like you to candidly assess them during your think time. If there are glaring gaps that cannot be corrected I would encourage you to act versus hope things will work out. Secondly I would ask you to honestly assess your personal competence around your competitors and list out the major macro and micro changes that effect your industry. If you have a short list I would urge you to spend more time examining your external environment to be able to capitalize on changes in your industry.

# Case Study: Joe—Savvy Veteran Tips

Every leader has moments of brilliance where a simple idea pops into consciousness. If we are smart, we write it down and follow it. I was in a group meeting one day, and we were having an idea exchange. Joe had a brilliant idea: he suggested we take all the really important nuggets of wisdom we have learned on our journey and write them down. Joe called it savvy veteran tips (SVT).

I took Joe's concept and sorted out some key ideas for you by chapter.

### Prelude: We Begin

- As you develop a relationship with your prospect, you become more genuine to him or her. Genuine leaders create referral machines.
- When things are not working, look in the mirror.

### Part 1: Who Are You?

- The best salespeople always say, "I want more help." They don't say, "I can do this by myself."
- What is special about you? Make sure it is in writing and can be shared with the prospect.

## Part 2: Building Relationships

- Leverage LinkedIn and invite every COI to view your profile.
- Know the leaders at each of your competitors. Don't be afraid to introduce yourself to the competition; every industry is small.
- Start conversations with open-ended, nonbusiness probes. "What are the latest updates from college for your three kids?"
- Don't let the optics of a competitor's offer interfere; focus on the total value of your firm and opportunity.
- What is the sweetest sound to prospects ears? Their own voices. In the first meeting, listen 70 percent of the time, and speak 30 percent of the time.
- Every time there is a change at a competitor's firm, you have an opportunity to call your prospects and reposition the opportunity at your firm.
- For charity-minded prospects, focus on your and your company's involvement in local communities. You know when to leverage this as you walk through their history in the industry, what's going on with their family, what they do for fun, and what their dreams are.
- Let your prospects know about the success statistics of prospects that are now clients. This type of validation provides a prospect with a comfort level that may get them to yes faster.
- Check yourself: if your prospect is saying no, you are not asking open-ended questions.

## Part 3: The Sales Process

- Mix up your mailings and calls. Don't keep calling all the same prospects each time—expand the pipe with new quality prospects.

- Spotlight other parts of your firm that help pre- and post-sale. Focus on the team concept.
- Always leave a voicemail that you would like to make that person's acquaintance.
- Keep things simple with your prospects. Identify what areas are green, what areas are yellow, and what areas are red. Celebrate green, work on yellow, and walk away if red cannot be fixed.
- When you choose to walk away from a prospect, don't be afraid to probe for referrals. You never know where opportunity will be created.
- Walk prospects through your websites, which strengthens the position of your company, its technology, and its competitive advantages.
- Saying no to a prospect who is not a good fit is a positive step for your local reputation and will help you in the long run. It is not a step back when you say no, it is a step forward and cleans up your prospect pipe.
- Less is more when you are speaking with prospects. Everyone needs to listen more effectively.

## Part 4: The Diversified Sourcing Strategy

- The only way to have a world-class pipeline to sell more is to start with a diversified sourcing strategy.
- Give in to the math of your job.
- Subscribe to every industry publication and daily e-mail to stay current on changes.
- Every time an external third party has good news about your company, send that news to your top-100 pipe with a hand-written note and a phone call follow-up the following week.
- When your company announces strong earnings, send it to your top-100 pipe to solidify the strength and stability of your firm.

- Put a note on your computer by your phone: "Get their personal e-mail address."
- Smile when you dial. We all have poor days. You are a terrific leader. Represent yourself and your firm well.
- Put a stop sign on your door when you are dialing your prospects. Let the internal team know that you need to block uninterrupted time in order for everyone to be successful.
- If you don't have corporate VIP trips, consider creating an experience that will get the prospect to yes.
- Understand the importance of developing your COI network.
- Cultivate your COIs carefully and in areas that are important to you

## Part 5: Meeting with the Client or Prospect

- Keep prospects alive by discussing different alternatives rather than focusing on one aspect of the sale. Keep your prospects thinking about you.
- Have a referral strategy that can help you to limit some of the DSS that isn't as much fun.
- Writing thank-you notes is a lost art that will get prospects' attention. Hand-written follow-up notes should be in a different color ink than the printed material so that your prospect knows you made the extra effort. Use stamps, not metered postage, with preferably wedding-style note cards to grab their attention.
- Leverage the team when you are making a large offer. Don't do it all yourself; create scale by using all available corporate resources.
- Have your prospects feel what it will be like to sit in the office, in the car, in the conference room, and in the airplane. Show them how great it will be when they say yes to you.
- Always have a written agenda for every meeting.

- Follow up with a hand-written note after each meeting; mention the next steps in that note.
- After a meeting, have a brain dump and capture all your notes in your CRM accurately before you forget the details.
- Based on past history, it is completely appropriate to say, "Yes, you are correct, that was how we were a few years ago. We have evolved. Let's spend a little time showing you what has changed."
- Objections are just a fun way of getting to yes. Embrace the objection and have fun cutting the objection down.

## Part 6: Evaluating Why Sales Aren't Increasing

- Log every conversation and meeting in a database that can be revisited for your next call or meeting. You can't remember a conversation from ninety days ago, but you add value when you reference past conversations.
- Time block one hour per day to call your warm and cold pipe.
- Walk away from a prospect who does not make sense. There are a lot of fish in the sea.
- Use what marketing materials your firm has—don't rewrite things. What matters is the follow-up phone call and face-to-face meeting.
- Before the second meeting or contact, send prospects something that positions the strength of your firm, like a testimonial from a client on your firm's website.
- When you are stuck, it is okay to say, "I've really enjoyed our time together, and I'd like to help you. What can I do to show you why I believe our company can help you move forward?"
- A prospect's greatest fear is saying yes, and then there is no follow-up. Help the prospect to understand what you will do after the sale.

## Part 7: Closing Thoughts

- You've got to have fun. Life is too short. If you are not having any fun, you can't sell more.
- Embrace the suck.

## Part 8: Bonus Coverage

- Learn about your company from the eyes of the consumer; surf all your public websites and consider what a client would think.
- Take your blinders off. You need to know what is happening at your competitors.
- Commit to attending external industry-wide meetings in order to learn about your competition.

You are special.
Make sure you can clearly communicate why you are special.
Finally, I believe you will be better off if you reread this book.
Create your master sales plan and then execute that plan.

### Activity

1. Please select one SVT from each of the eight chapters to work on.
2. Write down your SVTs in your CRM to share with your peers.
3. Revisit these SVTs each quarter and add, tweak, or modify as needed. Everything around us changes and evolves, so update your collective intelligence share.

- Please visit johnpierceconsulting.com to learn about other areas of interest that may benefit your firm.

- Please visit teleosleaders.com for more information on Dr. Frances Johnston.